Computer System Organization

The B5700/B6700 Series

Computer System Organization

The B5700/B6700 Series

ELLIOTT I. ORGANICK

Division of Computer Science
University of Utah
Salt Lake City, Utah

 ACADEMIC PRESS 1973 New York and London

ACADEMIC PRESS, INC.
111 Fifth Avenue, New York, New York 10003

United Kingdom Edition published by
ACADEMIC PRESS, INC. (LONDON) LTD.
24/28 Oval Road, London NW1

LIBRARY OF CONGRESS CATALOG CARD NUMBER: 72-88334

PRINTED IN THE UNITED STATES OF AMERICA

Contents

Preface

In 1961, the Burroughs Corporation began producing a line of large scale computers whose organization was radically different from conventional von Neumann computers. From the beginning, these machines have both stimulated and puzzled many who attempted to study them, partially due to inadequacies in the needed factual and expository literature about their internal structure.

The development began with a system called the B5000. A subsequent modification was called the B5500. In 1969, a major advance over the original system was completed and called the B6500. Since then, the B5500, which was still in production, and the B6500 were renamed the B5700 and B6700, respectively.

The structure of these highly innovative systems was widely publicized, but, lamentably, not well understood. Since 1968, however, when some technical descriptions of the B6500 system began to appear in the professional literature, interest has widened, reflecting I believe, a growing concern for the fact that conventional computer organization has remained relatively unstructured—with the objective of being "general purpose"—in the face of an increasing appreciation that certain information structures are characteristic of the computations we normally perform with computers. In short, the looming question has been: How can (or should) computer systems be organized to support, and hence make more efficient, the running of computer programs that evolve with characteristically similar information structures? (The body of this book is an attempt to make this idea more concrete.)

In many types of computer systems, increasing use is being made of virtual storage, which was one of the innovations of the B5000 System and has been an intrinsic part of the design of all subsequent Burroughs systems. I hope readers of this book will gain an historical perspective as well as a technical view of the Burroughs interpretation and implementation of this important concept.

I have aimed the book at an audience consisting of computer center directors, other computer professionals, and serious students in computer science who have an interest in the subject of computer organization. Although not designed as a textbook, this work may well serve for part of the reading in a senior or graduate course in computer system organization. Chapter 1 outlines the book's plan, so that one can decide, after reading this overview, if the material is likely to serve as suitable text material for such a course. I think it will.

A word of caution is perhaps in order for my readers. I have tried to avoid unprovable claims and have made a reasonable effort to delete from the manuscript unjustifiable adjectives of praise for the B5700/B6700 design. Nevertheless, this book retains a natural enthusiasm for the systems it describes. Complete objectivity in any study or exposition of this sort may be a goal that is achievable in an asymptotic sense only. Each reader must therefore apply his own "discount factor" in judging the merits of the opinions and conclusions that I have expressed here.

This book has benefited from the valuable assistance of many members of the Burroughs team who participated in the design and implementation of the B5700/B6700 systems. I especially wish to acknowledge the help received from David Bauerle, Stephen Billard, J. G. Cleary, Benjamin Dent, John Keiser, and Don Lyle. I also wish to thank the Burroughs Corporation management, especially R. R. Johnson and J. F. Kalbach, for the opportunity and support to make this study, and R. S. Barton, my colleague at the University of Utah, who served the role of effective catalyst. This book is published with the permission of the Burroughs Corporation. In undertaking the study on which it was based, I did not underestimate its difficulty, and make no pretense now that the book will prove as helpful to others as it has been for me. If indeed this effort does what I have set out to do, much of the credit should go to the reader, his patience, and his willingness to learn.

CHAPTER 1

An Overview

For the past ten years the Burroughs Corporation has been designing and producing computer systems whose organization and whose hardware/software designs have been significantly different and daring. These Burroughs systems have exhibited an organization consistent with a powerful semantic model for program execution, one that reflects a control structure (flow of control and addressing relationships) that is natural for, and hence one that facilitates, the execution of algorithms.

Spurred by the birth of Algol 60 [44], the last decade was one in which great strides were made in understanding and exploiting the potential of block-structured programming languages for representing complex algorithms, including large and small software systems [18, 21, 27]. Much has been learned about algorithms and ways to represent them in some fashion that would be optimal from the point of view of the man–program interface. With the exception of work on APL and related languages, nearly all recent work on syntactical and semantic design of programming languages has been based on the Algol 60 premise that (static) block structuring of algorithms, i.e., nested declarations, is a natural, if not requisite, form for the expression of complex algorithms (PL/1 [34], Euler [61], Algol 68 [60], Gedanken [51], PAL [62], . . . , Burroughs extended Algol [12]). With the exception of isolated computer designs (KDF9 [22], Rice #2 [52], and SYMBOL [15, 20, 53,

55]), few computer systems besides the Burroughs have yet to seriously cater for execution of algorithms expressed in such languages.*

Interestingly enough, the same Burroughs systems have been among the first to offer effective multiprogramming and multiprocessing—a goal of all of today's large computer systems and most smaller ones.

The Burroughs designers viewed the algorithms for their operating systems as inherently block structured and chose to code these algorithms in a language (an Algol 60 extension) that could reflect the structure. While to some others this choice may have appeared to impose unnecessary constraints for system development, the resulting products, measured in terms of throughput and flexibility (and related customer satisfaction), suggests that design "constraints" may really have been design opportunities [17].

The software/hardware developments of the B5700/B6700 progression have in the author's view anticipated (or at least kept pace with) the natural growth in sophistication of our view of algorithmic processes, and that view of algorithms has grown as a direct result of successful efforts of Burroughs and others to design, then further understand, then redesign, etc. very large programs, especially operating systems and information utilities.

It was common in the early 1960's to teach (in universities) that an algorithm is a sequence of procedural steps which, when coded in a higher level Algol-like language, could be structured as a set of nested blocks that defined the scopes of the algorithm's identifiers and dynamic resource requirements when executed on a computer. It may well be common in the 1970's, thanks to the efforts of computer science educators and researchers, and operating system and information utility designers [2, 4, 6, 8, 13, 14, 16, 24–27, 30, 32, 37, 39, 46–48, 54, 56, 58] that we shall teach programming by stressing that an algorithm is a structure (often nested) of interdependent, normally asynchronous tasks, the task being the entity that models the 1960's view of an algorithm. The coding of an

---

* The language APL [36] and close relatives such as LCC exhibit dynamic rather than static block structuring and as such are considered outside the scope of this book. Several research groups have reported on their efforts to build computer systems that cater for execution of algorithms in such languages [1, 7, 31, 57] and these are of interest.

individual task exhibits a structure that resembles in every respect
an Algol (or PL/1) procedure but might also have additional steps
to create, destroy, or synchronize with other such tasks.

The Burroughs B5700/B6700 "progression" appears to have had
as a major design goal the efficient execution of such algorithmic
structures. It behooves (us) educators and scientists to ascertain
the importance of this design goal and the extent to which Burroughs may already have achieved it—not just for the benefit of
its operating systems but, by simple recursion, for the benefit of
the system's users at any subsystem level. The principal purpose of
this book is to offer through informal exposition a hopefully revealing and fresh perspective of the B6700 (and by back reference the
B5700), its general design and design rationale, and its relative
potential as a computer system. The B6700 represents in some
sense a best display (i.e., an improved representation) of the corresponding ideas in the B5700. In other respects, such as memory
size and raw speed, the B5700 is simply a more limited version of
the B6700. For this reason no explicit discussion of the B5700 and
its comparison with the B6700 will be undertaken in this relatively
short treatment. By a proper whetting of appetites, however, it is
hoped to excite the reader into an activated state of inquiry for pur-
suing further study of the B6700, its predecessor, the B5700, and its
probable successors [2, 3, 8, 10, 12, 13, 14, 16, 21, 32, 47, 48].

The B6700 hardware/software architecture is interesting from a
number of different points of view—not the least of which are its
I/O hardware subsystem [48] and its information flow connec-
tions (I/O crossbar matrix) between static (memory) modules and
active (processor) units. Again, for the sake of brevity these aspects
are not discussed since we proceed on the assumption that such
features remain merely sidelights while the reader is still gaining
a clear understanding and an appreciation of the B6700's central
control structure, the why of it, and the how of it.

As early as 1964, the B5700 operating system was a productive
multiprogramming and multiprocessing system operating with
only a 32,000 word memory and one or two processors. Starting
from significantly different architectural designs, others have toiled
to achieve or exceed Burroughs' success, sometimes on systems
having far greater speed [18, 42, 43, 46, 56]. During this period

much has been learned about the technology and the underlying principles that govern multiprogramming and multiprocessing. Among the significant and perhaps best applied of these principles have been those based on the program property of *locality* and the consequent notion of the working set [23].

A program that exhibits a high locality of reference is one that "favors" a relatively small subset of its address spaces; i.e., in any given section of virtual time, an executing program is likely to make references within a comparatively small subset of the program segments. This subset is called the *working set*. (A more formal definition of locality and working set has been given [23], but for our purpose we are content with the above informal expressions.) Denning has shown that the number of independent programs that can be effectively multiprogrammed in a fixed size memory, i.e., without undue thrashing, can then be expected to increase as working sets (and the space required for them) decrease. Experience has shown [46, 59] that multiprogramming improves if the working sets of active processes can be (continuously) monitored and maintained in core memory when they execute. There are several points of interest regarding working sets of B5700/B6700 computations that are worth thinking (and perhaps speculating) about.

1. They exhibit strong locality. Working sets of such computations are therefore made relatively easy to maintain in memory while the task is active, because the procedures and the data components of the computation's information structure are the logical subdivisions identified by the programmer.

2. The effective size of the working set tends to approach the theoretical size [i.e., the actual amount of core required to contain the working set tends to approach the (theoretical) minimum amount of core required]. This is because:

    (a) the computation's local data structure which grows and shrinks as needed is always kept in core memory while the computation is active;

    (b) only those code segments of the algorithm which are currently being accessed by the processors must be kept in memory while the computation is active;

(c)   apart from certain system routines and tables shared by
all active computations, the only other portion of the
computation's information structure that must be kept
in memory while the computation is active is a dictionary whose entries point to all of the computation's
code segments. It is mainly the presence of this dictionary, normally small for small programs, which
makes the effective working set exceed the (theoretical)
minimum amount of core required.

3.   The processing cost for making demand insertions of new
items (segments), possibly to replace others that are no
longer in the working set, appears to approach lowest possible values. (By "lowest possible" we refer to the number of
logical addressing steps and not necessarily (physical) speed
of processing.) This is because when a nonpresent code or
data object must be obtained from secondary storage, the
so-called "descriptor" that is accessed by the hardware to
reach the desired target contains (directly) the address of the
target in auxiliary memory, and not an address of an address,
such as an address of a table that is to be searched for the
desired address.

If the author is correct in guessing that the B6700/B5700 hardware structure and selected storage representations offer these
attractive properties in the maintenance of working sets, it is small
wonder that effective resource utilization in these systems has been
notable, and that throughput relative to that of the less-structured
competing systems of comparable speed (and comparable I/O facilities, etc.) has been advantageous. Put another way, it becomes important to pursue the conjecture that architectural design based on
rational (semantic) models for the structure of computational processes, whose algorithms and records of execution are thought of
and represented as nested structures, leads to computer systems
with more effective resource utilization. The conjecture becomes
even more interesting if it is the case that related factors associated
with computer use, such as programming (and reprogramming) and
the cost of program information sharing, protection, etc., not only
do not suffer in tradeoff for the above multiprogramming advantages, but in fact strongly benefit from this design.

It is hoped that the reader will let his natural curiosity take him through the rest of this monograph and then on to further study of the B5700/B6700 so that he can draw his own conclusions.

The design for the remainder of this monograph is as follows: we give a stagewise (top down) exposition of the B6700 control structure to show how algorithms are represented and executed. For this purpose, a series of cases is exhibited, then discussed. Each case includes snapshots of an algorithm at several (interesting) points in its execution. The snapshot is discussed in terms of the revealing conceptual model recently proposed by Johnston [37] (called the contour model), which helps us to focus on the structure of the algorithm (the invariant code part), the structure of the current "record" or state of its execution, the state of the processor, and the interrelationships among them. The series of cases and discussions is designed to impart a cumulative (although by no means complete) understanding of the B6700's control structure as an implementation of a general model for algorithm execution.

As we proceed, we shall discuss several ramifications of this hardware and supporting software architecture, pointing out some of its relative advantages and limitations. Although no explicit comparisons with other systems are given, it is hoped that readers who study the Burroughs concept and implementation of segmentation, the resultant form of virtual memory, and the implications for certain types of controlled sharing of information will then find it easier to make their own meaningful comparisons with corresponding concepts in other systems (e.g., Multics [18, 46]). The same remark applies to comparisons that can be made with the tasking and interprogram communication facilities of other systems [4, 30, 42, 45, 56].

The case studies alluded to above are covered in Chapters 2–6. Chapter 7 considers one potential limitation of the B6700, a discussion of which is motivated in the preceding chapters, while Chapter 8 considers certain other limitations actual and alleged and the system modifications that would remove such limitations. Chapter 9 provides a more complete (and more detailed) view of B6700 hardware for those who will have found themselves ready for a deeper study.

The reader may have observed that this lengthy introduction is in danger of being concluded without mention of the word "stack." We remedy this situation here by observing that the hardware stack structures of the B5700/B6700 have been the key implementation device for achieving hardware support for efficient and controlled execution of algorithms. There can hardly be a reader of this book who is not somewhat aware that stack mechanisms exist in the B5700/B6700. However, many of our readers may not fully recognize how effectively Burroughs has been able to employ stack hardware to reflect an algorithm's static structure, and its execution record, and to build supporting hardware that exploits this storage representation for efficient execution, for recursive operating control, and for minimizing resource consumption.

CHAPTER 2

Block-Structured Processes and the B6700 Job

We start by grasping the concept of a B6700 *job,* which consists of a time-invariant algorithm* and a time-varying data structure which is the *record of execution* of that algorithm (Figure 2.1). The algorithm consists of a set of nonvarying code segments which are directly addressable (in the virtual memory sense).

The record of execution is a multipurpose data structure which at any given time defines

(a)   the execution state of the job, including values for all variables (scalar, arrayed, and structured);

(b)   the addressing environment (virtual address subspace) that a hardware processor serving this job may access, or possibly several (overlapping) addressing environments, in case it is appropriate that more than one processor be permitted to execute in the job at the same time (multiple activity);

(c)   the interblock/interprocedure/intertask flow of control history (e.g., chain of calls).

In its simplest view the hardware processor functions by maintaining a pair of pointers, an instruction pointer, *ip,* and an environ-

---

* In a more advanced view of a job, new code components might be attached to the algorithm during the course of its execution, but no component would vary (internally) in time.

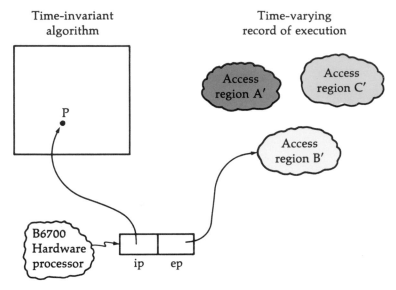

Figure 2.1   Snapshot of a B6700 job in execution. Schematic view No. 1.

ment pointer, *ep*, for referencing the accessible portions of the record.

Figure 2.1 suggests that the processor's instruction pointer is about to execute instruction *P* while the environment pointer, which points to region B' of the record, provides access to data in region B' during execution of *P*. Figure 2.1 implies that at some subsequent and/or previous point in time ep might point to any of the other access regions of the record.

Now, all B6700 programming is done in languages that are compiled in the block-structured sense,* explicit examples of which are Algol and PL/1. For this reason, the concept of disjoint access regions suggested in Figure 2.1 is, in an important sense, underconstrained. A more authentic view is given in Figure 2.2, which suggests that the B6700 processor's accessing environment is a type of union of access regions, say of C', B', and A'. The nesting of these regions mirrors the nesting of program blocks, each defining the scopes (i.e., range of validity) of program identifiers.

* Languages like Fortran may define only nonnested program blocks. Such languages can be regarded as degenerate examples of block-structured languages.

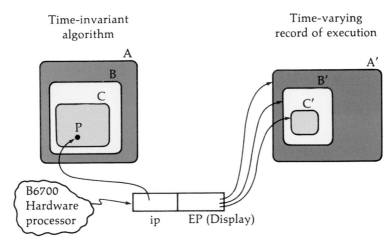

Figure 2.2   Snapshot of a B6700 job in execution. Schematic view No. 2.

Figure 2.3, for instance, shows the block structure and declarations of an illustrative Algol program. To the right of the program a "contour" schematic suggests an alternative representation that thrusts into bolder relief the scopes of the declared identifiers. Figure 2.2 can be regarded as a snapshot taken when the B6700 processor is about to execute an instruction at the statement labeled P of the program of Figure 2.3. This snapshot suggests that the environment pointer, now shown as a display, EP, which is a vector of pointers, will point to the record regions C', B', and A'. (The concept of display will be treated momentarily.) These access regions of course correspond respectively to sections (blocks) of the program whose corresponding scopes (contours) are named C, B, and A. [A prime-labeling convention (e.g., A' and A) is adopted to relate record contours to their corresponding code blocks.]

Cells associated with the identifiers c and d are contained in region C'; the cell for b is contained in region B', and the cell for a is contained in region A'. These cells are effectively accessed by name.

In the conceptual approach we may well view a reference to a, while executing the statement labeled P, to be a quest for the cell allocated for a. Such a search can be satisfied by an outward scan of the record regions C', B', and A', terminating on the first en-

Line
No.

0	**begin**
1	**integer** *a, b*;
⋮	⋮ } the real procedure, *rnd*
10	**begin**
11	**integer** *b, c*;
⋮	⋮
25	**begin**
26	**integer** *c, d*;
⋮	⋮
29	*P*: $a \leftarrow a \times b + c \times rnd(d)$;
⋮	⋮
34	**end**
41	**end**
⋮	
52	**begin**
53	**integer** *b, c*;
⋮	
	Q: ∿∿∿∿∿
⋮	
64	**end**
⋮	
72	**begin integer** *c, d*;
⋮	
91	**end**
⋮	
104	**end**

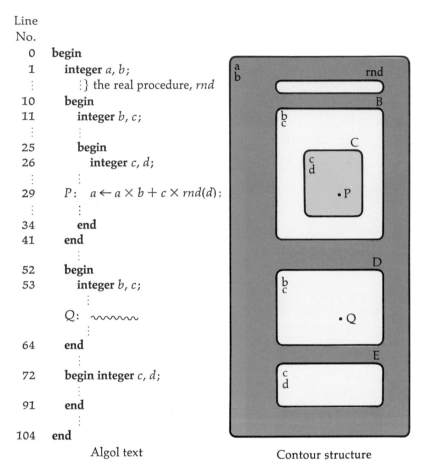

Algol text   Contour structure

Figure 2.3 Block structure and declarations of an Algol program with corresponding contour structure.

counter of a cell named *a*. Likewise, a search for *b* will succeed during a scan of B′. Note how the cell named *b* in A′ is therefore quite "invisible" (and therefore inaccessible) to the processor when it is executing the instructions at *P*. Figure 2.4 is an enlargement of the schematic record of execution shown in Figure 2.2 to show the cells allocated for all identifiers at that particular stage of execution.

Record of execution

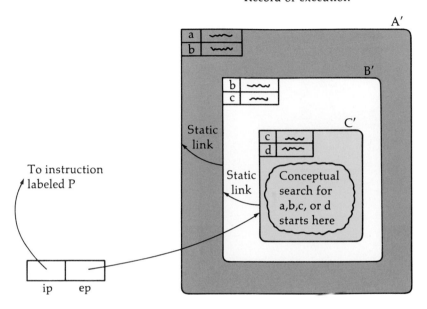

Figure 2.4   Record of execution while the program is executing at the statement labeled *P*. Contour model view in detail.

Of course, in the actual implementation no search is required because each identifier is renamed as an (i, j) pair, where i is a block height (nesting level in the program) and j is an ordinal number that refers to the jth identifier declared in the block [50].

A program may gain a second site of activity by asking for execution of a designated procedure as a task rather than as a subroutine. Figure 2.5 illustrates this concept in contour model terms and suggests how two (or more) processors may share the same code and (parts of) the same record of execution. The accessing environment for the second processor is defined by the display pointing to record regions D' and A', assuming the ip points to the instruction labeled Q shown in Figure 2.3.

Since region A' is common to the environments of the two processors, some locking discipline for achieving mutual exclusion is assumed to be employed. Programs that can support two (or more)

Invariant algorithm   Record of execution

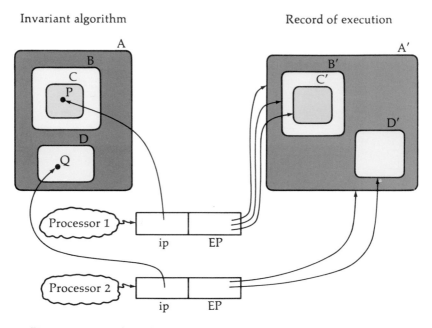

Figure 2.5   Snapshot of a B6700 job in execution with two processors. Contour model view.

processors have been called multiple activity algorithms [*38*]. Although an operating system is itself probably the best known and most important example of such algorithms, our case study approach is mainly confined to simpler examples.

A program that can support two (or more) processors need not have allocated to it more than one actual processor in order to execute effectively. A single processor can be shared among (scheduled to serve at) several sites of activity, first being assigned to execute at one site, then at another, etc., achieving the same effect as if there were concurrent execution at several sites but at greater elapsed time.

A program can still be viewed as one involving multiple processors (one per site of activity), as suggested in Figure 2.5, if one regards these processors as virtual (or pseudo) processors. Each such virtual processor is then simply a datum that defines a site of activity and that maps onto the hardware register structure of an actual processor whenever the latter is scheduled to execute at that particular site of activity. Put another way, an actual processor can be "passed around" among the virtual processors as needed, using an effective scheduling discipline. In the B6700 the "activation," i.e., assignment, of a virtual processor to an actual processor (and vice versa) is accomplished by a single instruction.

Tasks

Most of the simple programs we write (certainly those we have been accustomed to writing) never have more than one site of activity (at a time). The flow of control is sequential. The site of activity, i.e., the pair (ip, EP), changes dynamically, but one such (ip, EP) pair is sufficient to define the process' state of execution. Procedure calls and returns (recursive or otherwise), as well as coroutine calls and returns (recursive or otherwise) fall in this category of single site of activity. A second (or third, etc.) site is created when a program executes a designated procedure as a *task*. Completion of the task is one way that a site of execution may be terminated (destroyed). Tasks may also be temporarily suspended so they may later be reactivated.

The discipline surrounding the management of sites of activity, i.e., tasking, is discussed at some length in later portions of this book. In the terminology of tasking, the snapshot in Figure 2.5 can be interpreted in the following manner: The principal task is executing at program point P with access environments C', B', A'; a secondary or "offspring" task, spawned at some prior stage of the program's execution (perhaps as a call to create and execute a task at line 28 of the program in Figure 2.3) is now executing at program point Q with accessing environments D', A'.

CHAPTER 3

Basic Data Structures for B6700 Algorithms

3.1 INTRODUCTION

We are now ready for a closer look at the B6700 data structures
that are suggested in Figures 2.2 and 2.5. The code for a B6700
algorithm is segmented into blocks, as suggested in Figure 3.1.
Each block-structured language has its own syntax for use in de-
limiting such blocks. (Algol 60, for example, uses **begin, end** pairs
for program blocks and **procedure**, "; " pairs for procedure blocks.)
The code for each block is stored as a physically separate segment.
Each entry in the segment dictionary serves as a segment pointer
(or descriptor.) Only segments which are actually part of the specification of a site of activity (i.e., for an active processor) need be
present in physically addressable memory. [All segments of the
algorithm are, of course, present in the virtual memory of the algorithm. A "presence" bit in each segment dictionary entry is sensed
by the hardware address-formation mechanism. If this bit is off
when the descriptor is accessed, a hardware interrupt occurs which
delays further execution of the algorithm until the system locates
the desired segment (normally) in auxiliary storage and transfers
it to addressable core memory.]

When the flow of control moves from one segment to another
in the algorithm, the hardware accesses the segment dictionary to
acquire the base address of the desired segment as found in its de-

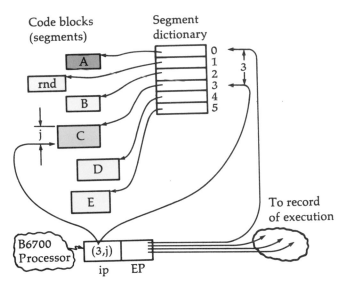

Figure 3.1 Showing how the code for an algorithm is physically segmented into blocks, each block pointed to by a descriptor in the segment dictionary.

scriptor. Thereafter each succeeding instruction in the same segment is accessed as an offset from this base. At first, we show the ip as a 2-tuple, the first component (3 in this case) being the offset into the segment dictionary, and the second component (j) as the offset within the segment. (Later the ip will be represented as a triple.) Thus, line "29" in Figure 2.3 can be thought of as being mapped by the compiler to the pair (3, j). Figure 3.1 suggests how the base address of the segment dictionary is determined, i.e., via a pointer that is pragmatically regarded as being part of the display "bundle."

The B6700 data structure for a record of execution takes the form of a stack structure. Figure 3.2 shows the stack structure for the record suggested in Figure 2.2. Stacks in this book are drawn so that they grow downward rather than in the more conventional (cafeteria style) upward direction. Nevertheless, we shall still refer to the cell containing the most-recently stacked element as the "top" of the stack and to the cell containing the least-recently stacked element as the base or "bottom" of the stack. This depar-

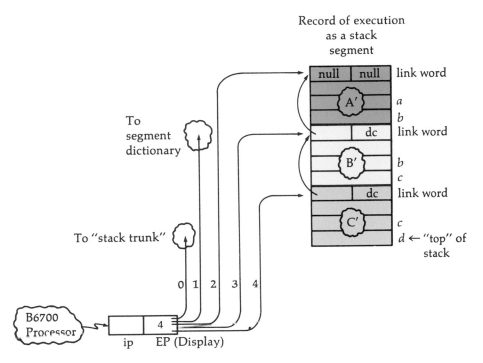

Figure 3.2 Snapshot taken while executing at point P in the algorithm of Figure 2.3.

ture from convention allows one to gain a more direct visual correspondence between the growth of the stack and the normal top-to-bottom instruction sequence of a block-structured program text.

There are three sections in the stack corresponding to the three contours of the current access environment for the instruction P. Randell and Russell, in the description of their Algol 60 implementation [50] call each stack section an *activation record*. Whenever execution enters a new block of the program, another activation record is allocated in the stack segment and appended (i.e., pushed) on to the top of the stack and back-threaded via *link words* to predecessor records in two ways. One thread (the static chain) shows the static linking of the records, i.e., to define the nesting of environments. The second thread (the dynamic chain), whose elements are denoted as dc, is not drawn explicitly but would, coincidentally, in this case be similar to the static chain. Upon block exit or procedure return, the accessing environment must be restored (reset) so that the topmost activation record designated by the EP bundle is that for execution in the immediately containing block or in the calling procedure, respectively. Links in the dynamic chain provide the information necessary for the processor to make this environment adjustment (including deallocation of activation records) when executing block exits and/or procedure returns.

As for the two *additional* display components, one points to the segment dictionary—as already mentioned—while the other points to the base of another area that is related to the work of the system's supervisor. This area, termed *stack trunk* [14] contains, among other things, the descriptors of all the supervisory code segments and system tables. For example, interrupt handlers whose descriptors reside in the stack trunk are accessed through the display pointer to the stack trunk. As a convenience, a simple, standard indexing scheme is used to distinguish the particular display elements. Thus, D_0 is the name for the stack trunk pointer; D_1 is the name for the segment dictionary pointer; D_2, D_3, and D_4 in this case serve as pointers to activation records that define the rest of the processor's accessing environment (i.e., regions A', B', and C').

Note, therefore, that the record level associated with the outermost block of any algorithm is always (arbitrarily) 2. The number 4 shown in the EP display box of Figure 3.2 simply signifies the index of the highest nonnull display pointer, there being 32 elements (D_0 through D_{31}) in the actual hardware display vector.

Figure 3.3 is a composite view of the algorithm, the stack structure, and the processors for the execution stage depicted in Figure 2.5. Examining this figure will provide us with additional preview of the subject of tasking that is treated in the next chapter. A few points may be noted.

The activation record associated with execution by the offspring task in the block called D is back-threaded via static link to the record for block A. Display register values are redundant but highly accessible copies of the static link values. Indeed, whenever a virtual processor is mapped onto an actual processor [i.e., whenever a processing unit is "awarded" to a task (site of activity) so

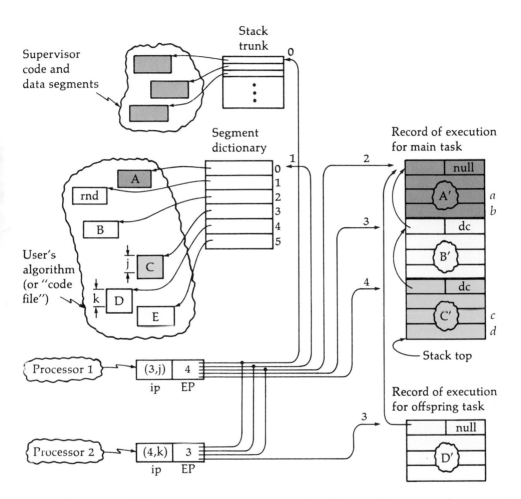

Figure 3.3 B6700 data structure showing the algorithm, and its structured record of execution, now consisting of two stacks, the segment dictionary, and the stack trunk. Display vectors of the two processors point to addressing environments "topped" by activation records for C' and D' at (display) levels 4 and 3, respectively. The first three display vector elements in each vector have identical values.

it can execute], the display registers for that processor are loaded by copying the static links. [Only the address of the topmost element in the display vector is not a copy of a static link. Only this address, therefore, need be saved as status from the display whenever an actual processor is awarded to another task within the same job or (to a task of another job).] Because record D' has no dynamic antecedent (also true of A'), its dynamic (chain) back pointer is (conceptually) null.

3.2 OPERAND STACKS

Our data structure view of the B6700 is still considerably oversimplified. For one thing, we have not considered the fact that every processor needs some scratch pad memory space for holding operands that are intermediate results needed to evaluate expressions. How much space is needed for such a processor-related purpose is dependent on the complexity of the expression. Compilers, of course, can determine in advance the amount of temporary storage that would be needed for any one simple expression evaluation. Note, however, that any *digression* in the middle of the expression evaluation, say to compute the value of some function to be used as an operand, will force some sort of a pushdown of the temporaries developed thus far so as to "make room" for new temporaries that may be required to compute a function value. For example, in the expression $a \times b + c \times f(g)$, where $f(g) = k \times g + u \times v$, if evaluation proceeds from left to right, then at the very least the temporary, t1, representing the value of $a \times b$, would have to be saved while the processor was producing a value for $f(g)$, evaluation of which requires its own temporary storage.

At the conceptual level the problem of where to save the temporaries may be solved by associating a separate pushdown stack with each virtual processor, as suggested in Figure 3.4. In any actual implementation of this concept, however, it is attractive to employ the top portion of the "current" activation record as an operand stack, and this is indeed the approach taken in the B5700/ B6700 implementation. We illustrate by again considering the statement labeled P in the program suggested by Figure 2.3. That statement is

$$P: a \leftarrow a \times b + c \times rnd(d);$$

where *rnd* is a random-number-generating function that is assumed to be a function procedure declared as a separate block (but not shown) in lines 2–10. Executing a reference to *rnd* causes compiler-generated code to create a new activation record, thereby saving the processor's temporaries for use upon return from *rnd*.

Figure 3.5 is an elaboration of Figure 3.2 to suggest the new condition of the stack segment while executing in *rnd*. Here we lift the curtain to reveal a few more of the details in the B6700 data structure. In doing so, we gain as a byproduct an introductory exposition of procedure calls, a topic that is developed further in the next two subsections.

1. First, notice that the activation record for *rnd* is indicated as containing *return information* (first entry after the record's link word). To return to a caller, a processor needs a *return label*, which is in essence a 2-tuple, of the form (ip, ep). Here ip is the position in the program that is one instruction beyond the point of call, and ep is a pointer to the (topmost) activation record employed by the caller. In returning to block C, the processor must also be able to reset other state variables, if any (e.g., various flip-flops), to their conditions prior to entering *rnd*. In the B6700 implementation, all this return information, including that which we have called the return label, is constructed and saved by the processor in the first two slots (words) of the activation record.

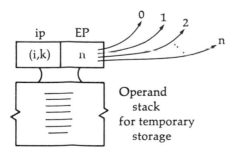

Figure 3.4   Virtual processor with an associated operand stack.

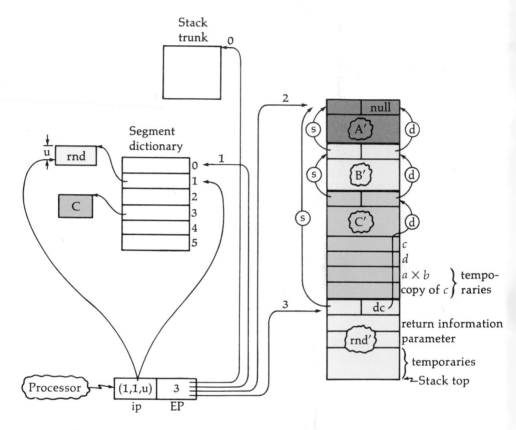

Figure 3.5 Executing the functional reference to *rnd*, which is assumed to be declared within block A of the algorithm. Lines marked ⓓ are dynamic links. Lines marked ⓢ are static links.

Note that ep of the return label is the value of the dynamic chain link (dc) indicated as part of the record's link word.

2. Second, notice that the ip is now shown as the triple (1, 1, u). It was previously shown as a 2-tuple. This added detail is given to clarify the way program point addresses are defined, but not necessarily how program points are accessed. The first element identifies the table holding the target instruc-

tion's segment descriptor (1 means segment dictionary; 0 means stack trunk). The next two elements identify the segment in terms of the offset (1) relative to the segment table (the segment dictionary in this case) and the offset (u) relative to the base of the target segment.

When execution "enters" a segment (i.e., when the hardware instruction *enter* is executed), one hardware register is loaded with the base address of the segment as extracted from its segment descriptor (found either in the segment dictionary or stack trunk) while another pair of hardware registers (not shown in our diagrams) is used as an instruction counter. (On each execution cycle, the hardware forms the byte address of the next instruction by summing the values of these registers.)

3. Third, observe that the activation record is dynamically linked to that of block C but statically linked to that of A, since *rnd* is declared in block A of the algorithm (shown in Figure 2.3). In contour terms, the accessing environment for *rnd* must be the one in which the record contour for *rnd* is (immediately) nested, and this contour is that of A. Observe how the EP display has been appropriately adjusted.

3.3 TREATMENT OF SYSTEM INTRINSICS

Suppose that *rnd* were not declared within the algorithm as suggested in Figure 2.3 but rather that *rnd* is a function recognized by the compiler as a system routine (referred to in Burroughs literature as a *system intrinsic*), whose code segment is pointed to from the stack trunk. Figure 3.6 shows the data structure that would then be developed for execution within *rnd*. System intrinsics are treated as if declared within procedures that execute at display level zero. Hence, system intrinsics always execute at display level 1 (one level higher than the level of their declaration). Figure 3.6 thus shows that the activation record for *rnd* is statically linked to the stack trunk. To avoid cluttering the diagram, the static link from A' is not shown. That link also reaches the stack trunk, though indirectly, via a link word in the segment dictionary.

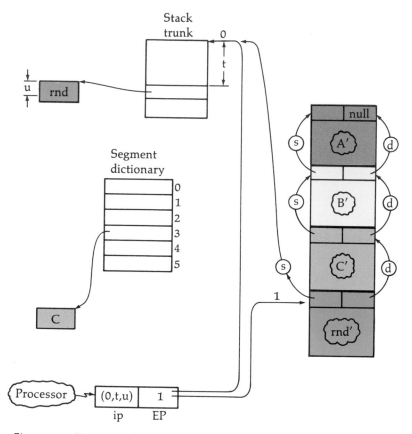

Figure 3.6 Executing the functional reference to *rnd*, which is assumed to be a *system intrinsic*. Lines marked ⓓ are dynamic links. Lines marked ⓢ are static links.

3.4 BLOCK EXITS AND RETURNS

Figure 3.7 shows the snapshot taken just after completing execution of the statement labeled *P*. In returning from *rnd* the top pointer of the EP display is again at level 4, pointing at C′. In effect, the activation record, rnd′, has been deallocated. The processor has stored a new value in the cell labeled *a* in the record A′. If any new temporaries are needed in the course of executing other state-

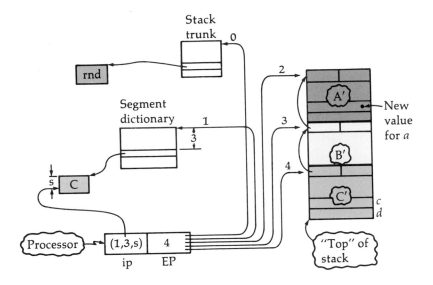

Figure 3.7 After completing execution of the statement labeled *P*.

ments in block *C*, they will be pushed onto the top of the stack as part of C' (where the record rnd' once resided).

Notice that a return from a function call (and the same would be true for a simple exit from a block) is accompanied by what can be interpreted as an act of deallocation. In Algol 60-like languages, this association of deallocation with returns (or exits) has its roots in the semantics of the language [37, 44, 58]. Note, for instance, that after return from *rnd* to block C the data items kept in rnd' are no longer "defined." Conceptually, such undefined items are no longer accessible to the processor. An act of deallocation, done by nullifying the processor's top display register, as in a simple block exit, is tantamount to making the record for that block inaccessible.

3.5 PROCEDURE CALLS—GENERAL

The approach to procedure call implementation has already been introduced indirectly in the foregoing discussions of Figures 3.5–3.7. Here we take a head-on look at the subject.

We select another model program, Figure 3.8, as a basis for dis-

Line
No.

```
0    begin
        A
1          integer j, n; real result;
2          array num[0: 99];
3          procedure sumit1(a, s, l, sum);
     sumit1
4              value s, l; integer s, l; array a[*]; real sum;
5              begin
6                  integer i;
7                  sum ← 0;
8                  for i ← s step 1 until l do sum ← sum + sqrt(a[i]);
9              end
9a         ;
10         [input value of n (≤100) and the set {num_j, for j = 0 step 1
                until n − 1}]
11         sumit1(num, 0, n − 1, result);
12         print(result);
13   end
```

Figure 3.8 Program for use in discussing procedure calls. Scoping lines at the left of the code are labeled A and sumit1 to correspond with the blocks of the program.

cussion. The program shows one explicit procedure call on the system's intrinsic *sqrt* and another on the declared procedure *sumit1*. Whether declared explicitly or implicitly, the compiler must generate a calling sequence that includes a reference to the target (procedure) segment. When executed, this reference is employed in an attempt by the processor to gain execution access to the target. Since it is the record of execution that defines the valid accessing environment for the processor, the compiler must specify the pointers to all called procedures such that during execution these pointers may be appropriately placed within the proper activation record used by the processor. The B6700 way of reaching this objective is suggested by a snapshot series shown in Figures 3.9–3.11 for the case where execution of the algorithm in Figure 3.8 is about to execute line 11, is about to execute line 9, and is about to complete execution of line 12, respectively.

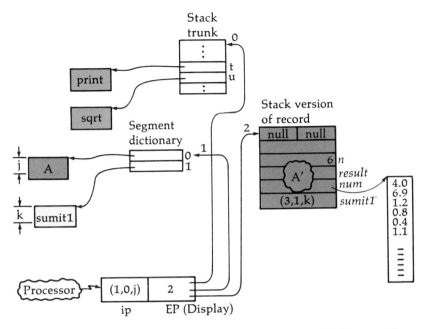

Figure 3.9 Snapshot of Figure 3.8 program execution just before executing line 11. Six data values for the *num* array are assumed to have been input as a result of executing line 10. (The symbols k and j represent entry-point offsets within the code segments for *sumit1* and block A, while the symbols t and u represent offsets within the stack trunk.)

Upon entering block A, the record A′ that is placed in the stack must (among other things) include pointers to all procedures that are explicitly declared in block A of the algorithm, i.e., the pointer to *sumit1*. Each such pointer is in essence an (ip, ep) label pair. The environment pointer component of the label defines the immediate environment within which the target procedure is to execute. In the B6700 representation, explicit ep values are, however, unnecessary, since the positioning of each procedure pointer within its appropriate activation record is tantamount to defining the addressing environments of the respective procedures.

Thus, the procedure pointer for *sumit1*, located in the activation record A′ and shown (3, 1, k), in essence specifies the display level

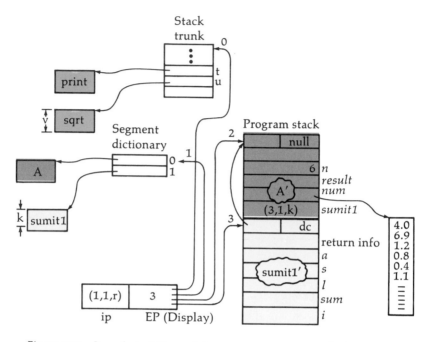

Figure 3.10 Snapshot of Figure 3.8 program execution just before executing line 9. (Symbols k and v represent entry-point offsets; symbol r represents the offset for the current instruction within the code for *sumit1*; and symbols t and u represent offsets within the stack trunk.)

(3) at which *sumit1* will execute, the segment number (1), and off-set (k) within the algorithm's code file. The segment number (1) gives the offset (always) in the segment dictionary where the segment descriptor for the target segment can be found. Readers should note that although the procedure pointer triplet, e.g., (3, 1, k) and the ip triplet, e.g., (1, 1, r) have for convenience been shown in similar syntax, their respective semantics are different.

In addition to the link word, called a *Mark Stack Control Word*, or MSCW in B6700 terminology, each activation record contains a word of return information, called a *Return Control Word* (RCW), immediately following the link word. The return label consists of an (ip, ep) pair, where the ip is contained within the RCW and the ep is in essence the dynamic link, dc, of the MSCW.

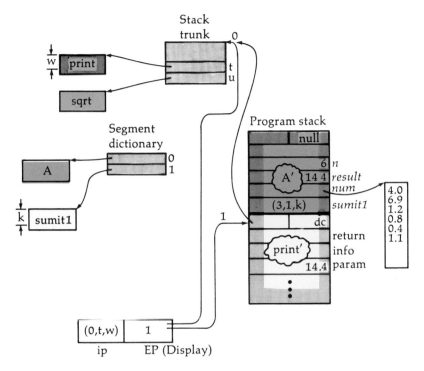

Figure 3.11 Snapshot of Figure 3.8 program execution just before completing the execution of line 12. (Shading for certain of the blocks is discussed in Section 3.7.)

3.6 HARDWARE INTERRUPTS AS HARDWARE-FABRICATED PROCEDURE CALLS

Perhaps the most significant simplifying design achievement of the B6700 has been the natural exploitation of the stack structure just described for the handling of hardware interrupts. Such interrupts were viewed conceptually by the B6700 designers to be merely unexpected procedure calls. This view has been fully realized.

When an interrupt signal is sensed by a hardware processor, it executes (through microcode) an enter instruction to a standard instruction address (ip) after first pushing a hardware-fabricated activation record onto the stack currently employed by that processor. The net effect is that when the "called" interrupt handler begins executing, it does so with a well-formed record of execution. That record is linked dynamically to the record of the interrupted procedure. Return information in the new record points back to the ip which represents the next instruction that would have been executed had not the interrupt occurred, and the formal parameters within the activation record have been given hardware-supplied values that define the nature of the interrupt.

The interrupt routine can examine the parameters and on the basis of their values call "specialist" handler routines for further processing, as required. If the special routines execute returns to the primary (system) interrupt handler, the latter will in turn execute a return to its "caller," which in this case is the interrupted procedure.

System interrupts need have nothing to do with the current program. The interrupt may, for example, represent an I/O complete signal that is quite independent of this computation. On the other hand, process interrupts (related to this task) such as arithmetic overflow, divide check, presence bit, etc. can also be processed effectively. In either case the interrupt routine executes at display level 1.

By using the present stack and fabricating ordinary procedure calls in the manner just described, there is minimum overhead cost expended in saving and restoring the state of the interrupted program. Figure 3.12 shows snapshots immediately after a system interrupt that is assumed to occur just before executing line 9 of the Figure 3.8 program. The (assumed) name of the system interrupt routine is *int*. Figure 3.12 may be compared with the snapshot in Figure 3.10 which is the situation immediately before the assumed interrupt.

3.7 SMALL WORKING SETS

A few other observations concerning the B6700 data structure are in order here. Note that the *num* array is not allocated as part of the stack structure. Only a descriptor to this array is kept (in

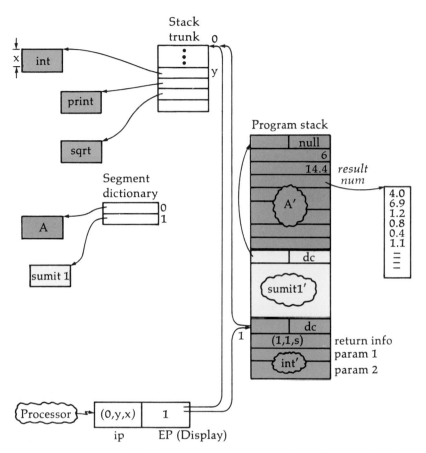

Figure 3.12 Snapshot of Figure 3.8 program executing after a system interrupt while the processor was getting ready to execute line 9. (See Figure 3.10 for snapshot immediately prior to this interrupt.) The interrupt procedure *int* executes at display level 1. Its activation record is statically linked to the stack trunk where it can access procedure pointers to other system procedures "declared" at level 0.

the record for block A). Since all references to the *num* array's elements must be made (indirectly) via the array descriptor, and since this descriptor has a presence bit that is sensed by the hardware, then the array itself need be present in core memory only when the program is making frequent references to it. By allocating data arrays and the stack segment separately, the stack can be kept small in size, thus minimizing the amount of core storage required for the record of execution in order to run the program.

This raises the interesting question: Just what portion of the job's address space does need to be present in core memory for effective execution? Well, of course, the answer must be phrased in terms of a particular snapshot of that job's execution.

Common to every job's execution there is some group of key supervisory procedure and data segments that will always be retained in core. These include the interrupt handlers, etc., memory allocation routines, perhaps some key I/O routines, all supposedly pointed to from the stack trunk. Apart from these "wired down" segments, what else?

We illustrate with the case shown in Figure 3.11. Shaded segments represent portions of the address space that must be kept in memory at the instant of that snapshot (for that program). Note the key roles played by the stack trunk, the segment dictionary, and the stack segment, in keeping the working set so compact. In essence, these three segments hold the descriptors (with presence bits) that point to all other segments that may be referenced by the job at this time. A descriptor is so formatted that if its presence bit is off, the remainder of the descriptor contains enough information to locate the missing segment (on disk) without first consulting intermediate tables of referenced information.

The stack trunk, though large, is actually shared by all jobs, and the segment dictionary is quite small for small programs, e.g., student programs. The minimum working set size, therefore, is determined mainly by the current size of the stack segment and the size of the currently executing program block. As a practical matter, however, the working set would also include those segments of the program and those system intrinsics that are frequently executed in the current flow-of-control pattern followed by the job—and also any arrays or portions thereof which may be frequently referenced.

Primary descriptors to arrays (and to other structured variables) are kept in the activation record. But the descriptors to substructures (also with presence bit sensitivity) are kept in intermediate arrays, i.e., "dope vectors" for the case of two-dimensional arrays. Treating arrays in this fashion tends to keep to a minimum the portion of an array (or other structure) that must be kept in core at any one time. Readers will note that many hardware paging techniques [23] also permit the subdividing of arrays into blocks, not all of which need be allocated concurrently in primary memory. But, such paging techniques are usually restricted to a fixed number of fixed-size blocks, whereas the B6700 system permits use of blocks whose number and size are arbitrary (and hence, blocks that can more closely match the actual structure of the array).

3.8 SHARING PROGRAMS AND DATA

To judge the incremental demand for core memory placed on the system by a job like that pictured in Figures 3.8–3.11, one needs to keep in mind several possibilities for program and data sharing in the B6700 (more sharing means lower incremental demands for core memory):

1. Two or more jobs may execute using the same algorithm (but on different data). For instance, one can picture several requests for printouts of current stock quotations (or current bank balances). Jobs for the several customers, each requesting that identical programs (code files) be executed, get to use the same segment dictionary and, of course, the same code segments. To be sure, the individual jobs have different execution stacks (records of execution). Since the code is pure and reentrant, there need be no synchronization among jobs that use identical "code files." The average working set size for such filial jobs (or rather, Siamese twins, triplets, etc.) tends to decrease with the size (number of jobs) of the "filial set."

2. Jobs may also share data arrays in three ways:

   (a) Descriptors for read-only data segments may be kept in the segment dictionary and hence shared by members of a filial set of jobs as with procedures. Depending on the block structure of a single job, such data segments may also be shared among tasks of the same job.

(b) Any data array, read-only or otherwise, can be shared among separate sibling tasks within a single job if their separate execution stacks were passed the same descriptor from their father task. Here again, such sharing, whenever it is frequent, serves to lower the average (effective) working set size of jobs or tasks.

(c) A task "budded" at any level has access to any descriptor owned by a (static) ancestor task at any lower level. It therefore has access to any information referenced by such a descriptor. This concept is illustrated in the next case study (in Chapter 4), where we consider two tasks within the same job that share the same array.

When data arrays are shared through different stack-based descriptors, special B6700 hardware operators are employed to give partial assistance in record-keeping, i.e., to see that descriptors to the same array are all properly updated whenever the location of the array or its attributes, e.g., its size, or its very existence, is altered.

CHAPTER 4

Tasking

4.1 CREATION AND COORDINATION OF TASKS

A specific example of a program that gains a second site of activity is illustrated in Figure 4.1. The overall objective of the algorithm in this figure is identical with that of the Figure 3.8 algorithm, but the internal structure is modified so that half the work of summing is delegated to an offspring task that functions asynchronously (e.g., can in principle function concurrently) with the principal task.

Lines 3, 5, 10, 14, and 16 reflect most of the new syntactical units required to achieve a simple, synchronized, tasking objective. At line 3 a variable, $ev1$, of type **event** is declared for use as the basis for synchronization. A matching formal parameter called *done* is declared in line 5 for the procedure *sumit2*. (Line 3 declares a null event that serves as a "syntactical dummy." We imagine it is required for matching *done* in the call on line 15.)

To request that *sumit2* be executed as a separate (but related) task, a new syntactical construction is needed. Burroughs Algol [12], for instance, employs the key word **process** to distinguish a task call (line 14) from an ordinary procedure call (line 15). The task call passes the actual parameter $ev1$ (by reference) to *sumit2*, so that the offspring task, an instance of *sumit2*, may signal the main task when the former has completed its work. The B6700

Line
No.
```
 0   begin
 1      integer j, n; real result1, result2;
 2      array num[0 : 99];
 3      event ev1, null;
 4      procedure sumit2(a, s, l, sum, done);
 5         value s, l; integer s, l; real sum; array a[*];   event done;
 6         begin
 7            integer i;
 8            sum ← 0;
 9            for i ← s step 1 until l do sum ← sum + sqrt(a[i]);
10            cause(done);
11         end sumit2
12      ;
13      [input value for n ≤ 50 and {num_j, for j = 0 step 1 until
            2 × n − 1}]
14      process sumit2(num, n, 2 × n − 1, result2, ev1);
15      sumit2(num, 0, n − 1, result1, null);
16      wait(ev1);
17      print(result1 + result2);
18   end
```

Figure 4.1 Program for use in discussing multiple sites of activity. Shaded sections reflect new syntactical units required to achieve a simple, synchronized tasking objective.

system intrinsic *cause* (on line 10) is used for this purpose. After executing the ordinary procedure call to *sumit2,* and passing it a null reference for the formal parameter, *done,* the main task executes a call to the system intrinsic *wait* (on line 16). *Wait* returns to its caller when and if the actual parameter, *ev1,* attains a value that may be interpreted as: "The event has happened." Upon return from *wait,* the algorithm calls for the printout of the sum of two values, *result1* and *result2,* each value representing half of the required work (the first half having been accomplished by the main task and the second half having been accomplished by the offspring task).

Variables of type **event** are structured. One field in this structure

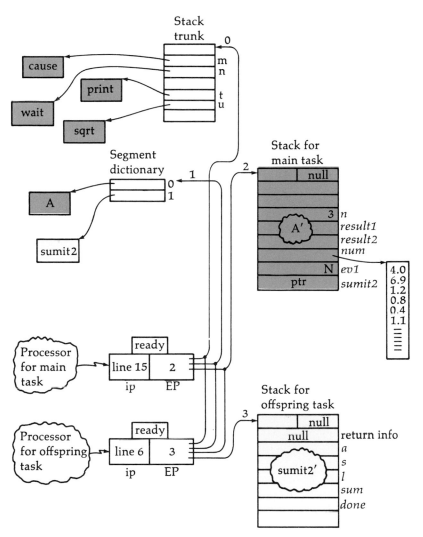

Figure 4.2 Simplified snapshot of the Figure 4.1 program just after creating the offspring task (at line 14). (The symbol ptr represents a procedure pointer whose form is discussed in Section 3.5.)

is a binary switch called the "happened" bit, which is set to *not happened* initially and later set to *happened* when the *cause* intrinsic is executed. The rest of the structure for an event variable is best explained in terms of several execution snapshots. These snapshots and the accompanying discussion are provided to illuminate the semantics of tasking.

Figure 4.2 gives a snapshot of the Figure 4.1 program just after the main task has created its offspring. The processor for the main task is pictured as about to execute line 15 of the program while the processor for the offspring is pictured as about to execute line 6. Each has its own EP display, the one for the offspring being—in this rather simple example—a copy of the parent's display to which has been adjoined a display element that points to the new task's "very own" stack at level 3.

The processors depicted in Figure 4.2 are virtual ones. They may or may not be currently mapped on to actual B6700 CPU's. In any case, they are *ready* to be so mapped, i.e., ready to run, whenever this form of physical activation can be accomplished. The execution state (variable) of a virtual processor, e.g., ready or waiting for some event to happen, can be thought of as attached to the processor, as suggested in Figure 4.2 or, as in Figure 4.3, to the stack of the task it now "serves."

Figure 4.3 reflects the actual B6700 implementation. The stack created for each new task begins with a task description area (of fixed size), following which is placed the first activation record. A combination of hardware and system software prevents access to this area except by supervisory programs. One of the key pieces of information in this special stack area is a thread (Q) by which a task may be linked to a list head that defines the queue state of the task. If the task is *ready*, Q thread is link-listed (lines marked ①) to a ready (R) head located in the stack trunk. Employing this list the system supervisor is able to choose (schedule) tasks to be run.

Figures 4.4–4.6 picture three possible snapshots of subsequent execution. In Figure 4.4 it is presumed that the main task has "speeded" through its work faster than its offspring, so the main task has reached and has executed line 16 while the offspring is just now reaching the *cause* at line 10. Figure 4.5 shows the effect

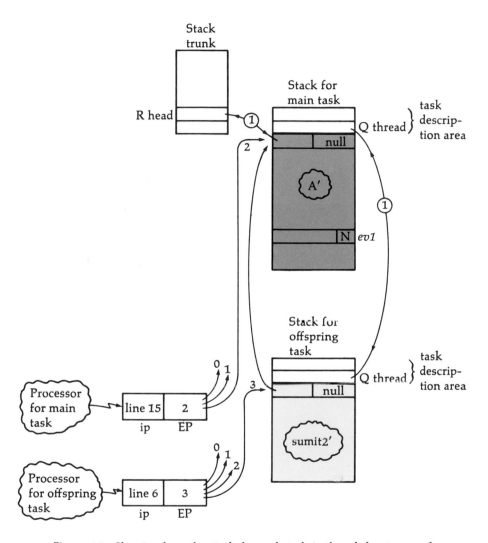

Figure 4.3 Showing how the stack for each task is threaded onto a ready list (lines marked ①), the head of which, R head, is kept in the stack trunk. Threading for each task is through a (one-per-task) queue thread (Q thread).

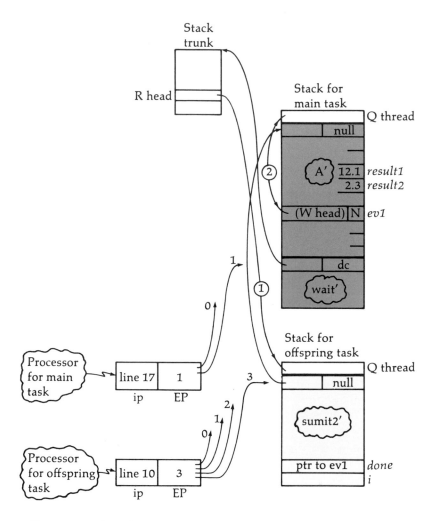

Figure 4.4 When the main task has executed the call to *wait* on the occurrence of event *ev1*, whose value is "N" (for *not happened*), the Q thread for the main task's stack is disconnected from the ready list and threaded onto a wait list, whose head word (W head) is in *ev1*. (See the line marked ②.) Only the offspring task about to execute line 10 remains connected to the ready list (line ①).

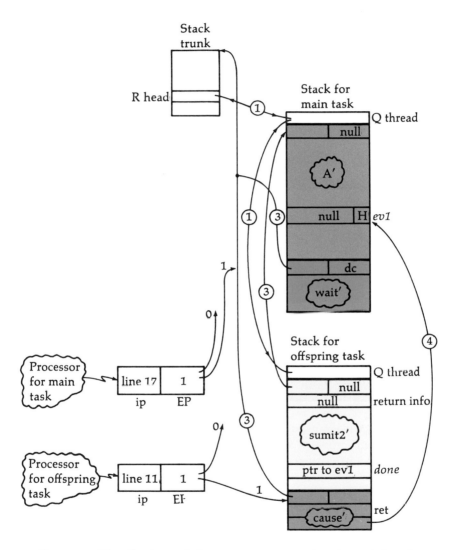

Figure 4.5 The offspring task, by executing in *cause*, has changed the value of the event variable *ev1*) to "H" for *happened* via the parameter *done* that was passed to *cause* as an argument. (See line marked ④.) The main task will now be able to resume by returning from *wait*. Lines marked ③ indicate various static links.

of the offspring having executed line 10 but not line 11. Figure 4.6 shows the effect of the offspring having executed line 12, i.e., exit from *sumit2*, which, in the case of a task, amounts to task termination, since the return label is null.

In Figure 4.4 we see what happens when a task executes a *wait* intrinsic and the named event has not happened ("N").

The main task has executed

$$wait(ev1);$$

When *wait* discovers that the value of *ev1* is "N," the Q-thread element is deleted from the ready Q (line ①) and linked into a wait queue whose head is a substructure of the *ev1* variable (line ②).

In Figure 4.5 we see what happens when a task *causes* an event. The *cause* intrinsic gets a copy of the value of *done* as its parameter, which, in turn, is a pointer to the (globally defined) variable *ev1*; *cause* has no trouble setting *ev1*'s happened state to *happened* (line ④). As a second step, *cause*, which is privileged to tinker with the Q threads, rethreads the main task's Q thread onto the ready list (line ①). Lines marked ③ in this figure are static links that define the respective addressing environments of the two tasks.

The return label for *sumit2* in the offspring stack has been marked null to suggest task termination when the processor for the offspring executes the procedure exit at line 12. In concept, such an exit is equivalent to a **go to** *null* statement. In the actual B6700 implementation the return slot of the first activation record of every task is not given a null value, but rather the entry point of a system control procedure (whose own activation record is then fabricated and pushed onto the stack trunk). This system procedure deallocates the task's stack (and any other resources associated exclusively with this stack) and thus terminates the task. Figure 4.6 is, therefore, a stylistic interpretation to connote the offspring task's demise.

4.2 TASK ATTRIBUTES

To gain greater control and/or communication among a family of tasks (those "started" by and including a common ancestor),

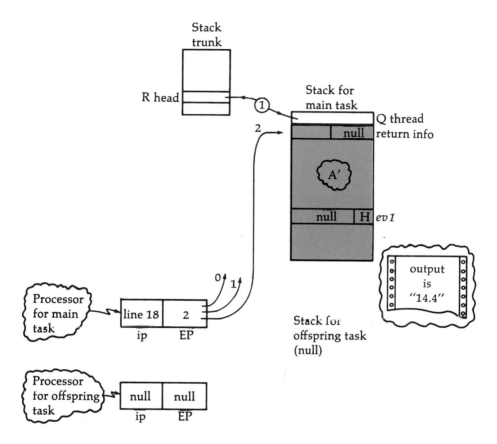

Figure 4.6 The offspring task has reached its terminus by executing line 12. Its ip and EP values are now (effectively) null. The main task has printed the results referred to in line 17 and is about to execute line 18 which will be its terminus (a block exit for which ip and EP are both effectively null).

each task is endowed with a structured *task* variable whose components define various attributes of the task.

The task variable is associated with the task at its creation and a syntactical facility has been provided to achieve this objective. Thus, strictly speaking line 14 of the Figure 4.1 algorithm was improperly coded since no task identifier variable was indicated to be associated with the created offspring task. A correct coding in Burroughs Algol would require that line 14 be coded, for instance, as:

> **process** *summit2(num, n, 2 × n − 1, result2, ev1) [charlie]*;

Moreover, an appropriate declaration, i.e.,

> **task** *charlie*;

would be inserted, say at line 2.5, to indicate that the identifier charlie is a variable of type **task**.

The task variable has a fixed structure so that it can be and is allocated into the task information area of the task's stack at the time the task is born.

Although the task information area is normally off limits in the accessing sense, tasks are afforded controlled access to the task variable substructure via what amount to "caretaker" intrinsics. Some task attributes are given initial values that are fixed for the life of the task. Others may be altered by the task itself, while still other attributes of a task may be altered only by certain other tasks of the family, e.g., parents.

A selected subset of the task attributes that are employed in the current B6700 implementation is discussed here. For convenience, the description is given in terms of the syntax now employed in Burroughs Algol.

Suppose a main task is coded to create an offspring and later make reference to task attributes of that offspring. Code such as the following might then appear in the main task portion of the algorithm.

```
Line
No.
2.5    task charlie;
 ⋮
14     process sumit2(num, 2, 2 ×  n − 1, result2, ev1) [charlie];
```

In addition, various attributes could be assigned to *charlie* before it is started. For example:

Line
No.
12.1 *charlie.priority* ← *5;*
12.2 *charlie.maxproctime* ← *20;* **comment** *in seconds;*
12.3 *charlie.stacksize* ← 2^8;

Lines 12.1–12.3 are intended to suggest that the system recognizes a subset of task attributes, initial values for which can be supplied by the creator task. Values for these attributes can then be noted and employed by the system's scheduling algorithm or other resource management modules. When any job is initiated, initial attributes for the main and/or only task of that job may be supplied by the user via control cards (i.e., at command level). In this way the user may specify attributes of his main task just as code in the main task may specify initial attributes for its offspring, or offspring for its offspring, etc.

The attribute *status* reflects the current execution state of the task [e.g., scheduled, running (active), suspended, terminated]. This attribute can be queried by any task in the family for which the task identifier (*charlie*) is "visible," e.g., its creator, itself, or any descendants for which *charlie* is global. In addition, these same tasks are able to write in the status variable, thus forcing *charlie* to be suspended, terminated, etc.

Some task attributes are provided so the system can log operational information, e.g., processor time and I/O time so far expended, time of day that the task was begun, etc.

Several key attributes have been defined for tasks to be used in achieving special interrelationships among tasks. Four of these attributes are *status, exceptiontask, exceptionevent,* and *partner.* They are explained here and their use is illustrated in Section 4.3.

Exceptiontask and exceptionevent are used, for instance, to alert a task, *A,* that there has been a status change for a given (descendant) task, *B,* or for any of a group of (descendant) tasks, *B, C, D,* etc.

To see how each of these attributes is employed, suppose we imagine that task *A* causes a change in its own status attribute, using the known task id, *myself,* e.g.,

myself.status ← *"suspended";*

The immediate effect of this statement is merely to request (of the system) a change of the task's status attribute to a new code value. But, eventually, the system's scheduling machinery will take note of this request (when it next attempts to ready task *A*, assuming some time-sharing or multiprocessing discipline is governing) at which time the system will change the status value of task *A* and will actually suspend task *A*. (Only another task that is apprised of this suspension can reverse this action.)

The system reacts as follows upon noticing a change in task *A*'s status: Task *A*'s exceptiontask attribute, which is interpreted as a task identifier, is used by the system to *notify* that target (task) of the status change for *A*. Let the target task so identified be task *B*, which is perhaps the immediate ancestor of task *A*. Now, task *B* has associated with it its own structured task variable, one of whose components is *B.exceptionevent*. This component is an event variable (automatically declared and initialized to "N" by the system). Upon noticing a change in status for *A*, the system *causes B.exceptionevent*, i.e., the exceptionevent "belonging" to the task designated by *A.exceptiontask*. If *B* had been waiting for this event, *B* would now be readied and allowed to resume. Note that any other tasks that happen to be Q-threaded, i.e., wait-listed, on *B.exceptionevent* will be correspondingly alerted. Thus, the net effect of a *myself. status* change can be to alert a series of other tasks (broadcast) that may be waiting to learn of this occurrence. In Chapter 6, when we discuss software interrupts, we will see then that an alternative effect of *cause*ing an exceptionevent can be to have the notification take the form of interrupts.

In the B6700 implementation, the task that starts *charlie* (or any task that can "see" *charlie*'s task variable) can act like *charlie*'s supervisor or big brother, because such a task (besides *charlie* himself) can write as well as read *charlie*'s status attribute. Let *pete* be any task that can see *charlie*'s task variable. Then:

1. Depending on *charlie*'s status, *pete* can activate, suspend, or terminate *charlie*.

2. If *charlie* has been suspended by virtue of executing a condition handler invoked by some hardware-detected processing

fault, e.g., a floating point overflow, *pete* can read some of *charlie's* attributes and attempt a diagnosis of the trouble. Among the attributes that are useful for such diagnosis is the *stoppoint* attribute, which is the ip of the (*charlie's*) last executed instruction.

We see that *pete* is able to control *charlie's* execution state via *charlie.status* and *charlie* can alert *pete* to a change in the former's status.

If no initial value is assigned to *charlie.exceptiontask*, then *pete*, the task that starts *charlie*, is the exceptiontask for *charlie* by default. But note that *charlie.exceptiontask* can be altered afterwards, either by *pete* or by *charlie* himself. Thus, in the latter case, a statement like

$$myself.exceptiontask \leftarrow brothertom;$$

is a way for *charlie* to let the task named *brothertom* "look after him." The intent of such a statement is equivalent to, "In case I am suspended, do not tell my parent, tell brothertom." In this way, two or more tasks can establish one another as watchguard of one another (e.g., *A* is the exceptiontask for *B*, and vice versa).

The *partner* attribute enables tasks to relate to one another not as asynchronous computations but as coroutines, i.e., synchronous computation. For example, tasks *A* and *B* can act as coroutines if *A*.*partner* = *B* and *B*.*partner* = *A*. Then, when task *A* executes a statement like the Burroughs Algol:

continue;

the effect is to stop executing *A* and *resume* executing *B* at the point that *B* last executed a **continue** statement. Since the partner attribute is read/writeable, any one task can select a new partner (as in a dance?) by reference to a task variable when it next gets a chance to execute.

Three or more tasks can relate to one another as coroutines, for instance, forming a ring (or daisy chain), e.g., *A*.*partner* ← *B*, *B*.*partner* ← *C*; *C*.*partner* ← *A*.

One scheme for coroutine communication has been implemented so that a programmer can override the partner attribute by naming any task variable in the continue statement. Thus,

continue(C);

means relinquish control to C as a coroutine (regardless of who my current partner happens to be). In such a case, C would resume executing at the point following the last **continue** that it executed.

4.3 ILLUSTRATIVE PROBLEM

Here we shall select a simple problem whose solution "invites" use of tasking and thus illustrates some possible uses for task variables and a number of the task attributes whose semantic interpretation was given in the preceding section. Readers who were satisfied with the previous explanations may skip over this section without loss of continuity.

4.3.1. The Problem*

Consider three identical stream controllers that interact with one another in a manner to be stated below. Each controller monitors flow of a stream, which may be thought of as a fluid such as oil or water (or as a granulated material such as grain, or as a stream of numbers). Each controller permits the stream it controls to flow into a tank (or bin or accumulator). The controller is capable of knowing the cumulative flow into its tank because it is able to continuously meter the stream quantity that is admitted.

What is of interest is that each controller tries to maintain an input rate that is related to the input rates maintained by the other controllers. In short, by "cooperating" with one another, the controllers try to admit the same stream quantities (approximately, that is) that the other controllers are admitting to their respective tanks.

Write a computer program that models this situation by assuming that the fluid being controlled in any one stream is a series of

* Approximately as the author recently posed it to some undergraduate students.

integers, read at (an essentially) constant rate from an input file. For simplicity, also assume that a controller A meters its stream simply by generating the sum of the integers that it has input (thus far). Call this sum SA.

Controller A is capable of knowing what has been input (in the cumulative sense) by the other controllers because it is able to access SB and SC, the sums generated by controllers B and C.

Then controller A can periodically check to see if the condition

$$SA > SB \text{ and } SA > SC = \textbf{true} \tag{1}$$

is satisfied, and when it is, shut off the flow into its tank. In so doing, we assume that A can effectively notify at least one of the other two controllers of its action (suspension). If condition (1) is not satisfied, A can continue to meter "fluid'" into its tank.

We picture that each controller works in the manner described above. A controller A should shut down completely (i.e., terminate operation) when it has sensed that $SA > INMAX$, where $INMAX$ is some given limit. Satisfying this condition should also signal termination of the computation as a whole. Prior to termination however, there should be (periodic) output which displays the triple (SA, SB, SC) whenever any controller finds that it must shut off its stream temporarily, i.e., whenever the controller finds that condition (1) is satisfied.

4.3.2. Three Possible Solutions

Figures 4.7–4.9 are three possible solutions. Readers are invited to examine these and then develop (at least) one or more of their own. Figure 4.7 shows a way of using status and exceptiontask attributes. In Figure 4.7 notification is always round robin, i.e., A to B, B to C, and C to A, when a given controller finds that it is "ahead of" the other two. Notification is achieved by forcing the target task out of its suspended state. A task that has suspended itself, as on line 12 of Figure 4.7, can be unsuspended* only by help from another task—normally its exceptiontask, as on line 11 of Figure 4.7.

* The literals *"suspended"* and *"wakeup"* are intended to represent the integer codes that are interpreted by the software to mean suspended and unsuspended, respectively.

Line
No.

```
 1    begin
 2      integer SA, SB, SC, INMAX; task A, B, C; event doneABC;
 3      procedure controller1(s1, s2, s3, n, done);
 4        value n; integer s1, s2, s3, n; event done;
 5        begin
 6          integer VAL; label L;
 7          L: if s1 > s2 and s1 > s3
 8            then begin
 9              [print values of s1, s2, and s3 in appropriate columns
10                  of a table, based on the value of n];
11              (myself.exceptiontask).status ← "wakeup";
12              myself.status ← "suspended";
13              go to L; end
14            else begin
15              [input a value of VAL from input file n];
16              s1 ← s1 + VAL;
17              if s1 < INMAX then go to L else cause(done);
18                end
19          end controller1
20        ;
21      A.exceptiontask ← B;
22      B.exceptiontask ← C;
23      C.exceptiontask ← A;
24      [input a value for INMAX];
25      SA ← SB ← SC ← 0;
26      process controller1(SA, SB, SC, 1, doneABC)[A];
27      process controller1(SB, SA, SC, 2, doneABC)[B];
28      process controller1(SC, SA, SB, 3, doneABC)[C];
29      wait(doneABC);
30    end
```

Figure 4.7 Stream controller problem programmed using asynchronous tasks. Note the use of exceptiontask, exceptionevent, and status attributes. Mutual notification among tasks *A*, *B*, and *C* is round robin.

In Figure 4.8, notification is to the controller that is "farthest behind." It is not obvious which of the two strategies (Figures 4.7 and 4.8) is better from the point of view of trying to keep consistently as many as two controllers at a time busy inputting stream

```
Line
No.
  1    begin
  2       integer SA, SB, SC, INMAX; task A, B, C; event doneABC;
  3       procedure controller2(s1, s2, s3, n, done, t2, t3);
  4          value n; integer s1, s2, s3, n; event done; task t2, t3;
  5          begin
  6             integer VAL; label L;
  7             L: if s1 > s2 and s1 > s3 then begin
  8                [print values of s1, s2, and s3 in appropriate column of a
  9                   table, based on the value of n];
 10                if s2 < s3 then t2.status ← "wakeup"
 11                         else t3.status ← "wakeup";
 12                myself.status ← "suspended";
 13                go to L; end
 14                else begin
 15                [input a value of VAL from input file n];
 16                s1 ← s1 + VAL;
 17                if s1 < INMAX then go to L else cause(done);
 18                end
 19          end controller2
 20       ;
 21       [input a value for INMAX];
 22       SA ← SB ← SC ← 0;
 23       process controller2(SA, SB, SC, 1, doneABC, B, C)[A];
 24       process controller2(SB, SA, SC, 2, doneABC, A, C)[B];
 25       process controller2(SC, SA, SB, 3, doneABC, A, B)[C];
 26       wait(doneABC);
 27    end
```

Figure 4.8 Stream controller problem programmed using asynchronous tasks. (Programming is similar to that of Figure 4.7.) Mutual notification among tasks A, B, and C is based on helping the hind-most.

values—given that there are at least two hardware processors available for service. (Of course, at the very outset, all three controllers are allowed to start working concurrently, but very quickly it will be the case that the average number of controllers working drops below two.) Readers may find the problem of selecting a notification strategy an interesting problem for study.

Figure 4.9 displays what might be regarded as a logically simple

```
Line
No.
 1    begin
 2       integer SA, SB, SC; task A, B, C;
 3       procedure controller3(s1, s2, s3, n, t2, t3);
 4          value n; integer s1, s2, s3, n; task t2, t3;
 5          begin
 6             integer VAL; label L;
 7             continue;
 8             L: if s1 > s2 and s1 > s3 then begin
 9                [print values of s1, s2, and s3 in appropriate columns of a
10                   table, based upon the value of n];
11                if s2 < s3 then continue(t2) else continue(t3); go to L; end
12             else begin
13                [input a value of VAL from input file n];
14                s1 ← s1 + VAL;
15                if s1 < INMAX then go to L else continue;
16                end
17          end controller3
18       ;
19       SA ← SB ← SC ← 0; comment the following line is actually
             superfluous;
20       A.partner ← myself; B.partner ← myself; C.partner ← myself;
21       call controller3(SA, SB, SC, 1, B, C)[A];
22       call controller3(SB, SA, SC, 2, A, C)[B];
23       call controller3(SC, SA, SB, 3, A, B)[C];
24       continue(A);
25    end
```

Figure 4.9 Stream controller problem using coroutines in place of asynchronous tasks. Note use of the partner attribute.

solution—using coroutines. If on the average only one processor is available for service, the coroutine approach may prove attractive. Note that when first *called*, the coroutine is programmed (in *controller3*) to **continue** (back to the main task) as soon as it has been created. In this way, the main task is able to set up (establish an addressing environment for) all three coroutines before starting up any of them.

Upon completion of this setup, the main task **continue**s to coroutine A (line 24). From here on out, control moves sequentially (and synchronously) among tasks B, C, and A, using a help-the-hindmost strategy, until one of the coroutine controllers fails the test in the line 15 **if** statement and **continue**s to its partner. Since all three coroutines have the main task as partner-in-common, then, whosoever issues the **continue** on line 15 *causes* the main task to resume at line 25 and end it all.

Several other read/write task attributes have been defined for use as shared data cells, purely for the convenience of the programmer, e.g., for sending short messages between tasks. For instance, one such attribute called *locked* is of type **Boolean**; another, called *taskvalue*, is of type **real**.

The foregoing survey of task variables, their attributes and uses for intertask control and communication is admittedly incomplete. Nevertheless, it is hoped readers can see the powerful tools offered to the programmer for construction of complex subsystems having families of tasks. A good bit of the versatility and control seems to be derived by virtue of the block structure nature of the program in which such task families are coded. The B6700 hardware is, of course, keyed to this block structure.

CHAPTER 5

Stack Structure and Stack Ownership

5.1 THE CRITICAL BLOCK CONCEPT

Consider a task family such as that depicted in Figure 5.1 and the treelike stack structure that represents the records of execution. The statically linked set of activation records defining the accessing environment of any one (offspring) task extends over two or more separate stacks.

The highest display-level portion of the environment for an offspring task depicted in this figure is found in the stack associated with that task. These access regions connect to access regions at lower display levels through as many separate stacks as are required to include the root or main stack of this job. Only the first of these stacks (for which the display level is highest) is directly associated with the given task. It is the one that uniquely identifies or associates with the virtual processor that executes this task. One may choose to speak about the task as *owning* this stack of highest display level. Correspondingly, the other stacks in this task's accessing environment con be thought of as being owned, respectively, by each of the task's ancestors. Thus, in the example of Figure 5.1, the m.a.a-stack can be said to be owned by the task named m.a.a; the m.a-stack, which holds part of m.a.a's access environment, is owned by m.a, etc. It is also true that the stacks making up one accessing environment for a task need not all be

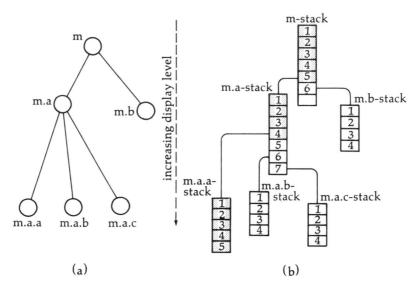

Figure 5.1 Family trees and corresponding B6700 stack structure. Shaded activation records might represent the accessing environment for task m.a.a at some stage of its execution. Numbers inside the individual stacks are used (in the text) to reflect individual activation records. (a) A job's (family) tree of tasks. (b) B6700 stack structure schematic.

interrelated in the ancestral (or father–son) sense that was discussed in Chapter 4. The discussion in this section is deliberately simplified, however, by making this assumption for the case illustrated in Figure 5.1. (In the following paragraphs, therefore, the term, parent or ancestor, is to be interpreted as antecedent in the static link sense and, coincidentally, also in the tasking sense.)

Not all of each stack owned by an ancestor need be part of a given task's accessing environment. Thus, in Figure 5.1 only activation records 4, 3, 2, and 1 of the m.a-stack are assumed to be statically linked into m.a.a's addressing environment.

If a task such as m.a.a is to execute to completion, its accessing environment, whatever it may be, must be preserved throughout the duration of that execution. An interesting question arises, however, when we consider the situation that could occur, say, if task m.a were terminated before task m.a.a completed its chores. If termination of a task is accompanied by deallocation of its owned stack (m.a-stack), then part of m.a.a's accessing environment would disappear, leaving m.a.a unable to compute properly since many of its globally defined values would be lost. (The same problem could, of course, be rephrased in terms of a termination of task m.)

A somewhat more subtle situation might also give rise to a loss of (part of) m.a.a's accessing environment. Suppose task m.a executes a series of procedure returns (asynchronous of any action on m.a.a's part) such that activation records 7, 6, and 5 in m.a-stack are now deallocated. This is no problem as far as m.a.a is concerned. But, at the instant record 4 is also deallocated, m.a.a will have been catastrophically affected. The block or procedure that m.a executes, whose activation record is record 4, is called m.a.a's *critical* block (and record 4 called a *critical activation record*) relative to m.a. Once the record for a task's critical block (a record in its parent's stack) is deallocated, the offspring can no longer execute effectively. We see, therefore, that what is really critical for a dependent task to be able to continue is not whether the parent is merely alive but whether or not the parent is still executing in the critical block (or in one of its dynamic descendants). In order to simplify the remainder of this discussion on tasking, we shall deliberately couch our remarks simply in terms of the life or death existence of the parent (i.e., as if the stack for the parent never has more than one activation record in it).

One of two stack management disciplines is open to the system designer to prevent a task from executing with a (partially) deallocated accessing environment.

1.   Preserve a stack—even after the demise of the task that owns it—so long as at least one of the offspring tasks "lives" (see, for example, papers by Johnston [37] and Berry [6] for a full discussion of the "retention" discipline), or

2.   When a task terminates (or is terminated), then (also) terminate all its offspring tasks. With this approach, not only could the stack owned by a task that is being terminated be

safely deallocated, but the stacks of any offspring tasks could be deallocated as well. The current B6700 implementation follows discipline 2 for two reasons:

(a) *Philosophical.* Since offspring tasks are regarded as dependent rather than independent activities, it would seem that their separate existence (after the demise of their immediate ancestor) cannot be justified. If a task must have a truly independent existence, it can and should be initiated and executed as a separate job (or as part of a separate job) in the system. (Any program can initiate a separate job.)

(b) *Sociological.* The semantic specification of tasking as currently defined in PL/1 follows discipline 2. Some attempt to maintain compatibility with the tasking semantics of this widely used language, which was historically the first to include detailed specification for tasking, seems appropriate.

In the B6700 implementation the tasking is, of course, a system-provided facility so it is available to programmers in a number of the higher level languages offered as part of the system software.

5.2 DEPENDENT VERSUS INDEPENDENT TASKS

The matter of which discipline to choose is not entirely academic. For example, Figure 5.2, a variant of the program in Figure 4.1 exhibits a simple case where an ancestor may well complete its work (terminate) before its offspring does, leading to a potentially disastrous consequence. In the new example program, the main task creates an offspring to execute the procedure *sumit3*, which does the same work as *sumit2*, but prints its result rather than "reporting" it to its ancestor (by assigning the result to a globally defined argument and notifying him via *cause*).

In an environment of multiprogramming on a multiprocessor sys-system, whether the main task of Figure 5.2 will complete before or after the offspring completes its task is indeterminate. As can be seen, there is no explicit programming to synchronize execution

```
Line
No.
 0    begin
 1       integer j, n;
 2       array num[0 : 99];
2.5      task charlie;
 3       procedure sumit3(a, s, l, id);
 4          value s, l, id; integer s, l; array a[*]; string id;
 5          begin
 6             integer i; real sum;
 7             sum ← 0;
 8             for i ← s step 1 until l do sum ← sum + sqrt(a[i]);
 9             print(id, sum);
10          end sumit3;
11       [input value of n (≤50) and {num_j, for j = 0 step 1 until
              2 × n − 1}]
12       process sumit3(num, n, 2 × n − 1, "uppersum") [charlie];
13       sumit3(num, 0, n − 1, "lowersum");
14    end
```

Figure 5.2   A program with two tasks that are not synchronized.

of these two tasks, nor in principle is there any need for synchronization in this case. Nevertheless, if discipline 1 were followed, the relative speeds of the two tasks would be immaterial, whereas if discipline 2 were followed, the program would work well if the offspring task finishes first, or if it finishes in a "dead heat" with its ancestor, but works poorly (i.e., not at all) if the main task finishes first. (For, if main finishes first, the activation record at level 2, which contains key values and pointers needed by sumit3, would be lost.)

Ultimately, a choice of stack-management disciplines must rest on what is meant by task dependence and independence. It can be argued that the Figure 5.2 program is a good example of the misapplication of a useful tool, i.e., that sumit3 should have been executed not as a dependent task but as an independent task, i.e., as another job. In the B6700 implementation, a task of one job can indeed start up a new job and hand over to that new job a set of parameters (call-by-value only) in such a way as to make the new job's existence independent of the subsequent (life or death) history of the first job.

It must be conceded, however, that as of 1972 there has hardly been amassed any abundance of applications programming experience with tasking for use as a pragmatic basis in deciding on the type of stack management discipline that should be used—whether using PL/1 or any other programming language. It turns out that either discipline is in fact relatively simple to implement in the B6700 system for the following reason:

As currently implemented, execution of a block exit will sometimes be achieved by a compiler-generated call to a system routine called *blockexit*. (This will occur when, at compile time, it is evident that system action at block exit will be wanted.) One of the responsibilities of this routine is to interrogate a variable associated with the given block, called criticalblockcount (*cbc*), which is a count of still-active offspring tasks created during this activation of the block being exited. The condition, $cbc > 0$, is currently treated as a programmer error, and the exiting task and all its offspring tasks are terminated. Of course, this termination is accompanied by the display of a suitable error message. By requiring that all block exits be compiled as calls to the blockexit routine, stack retention discipline could be implemented simply by treating the condition, $cbc > 0$, as an indication that the block-exiting task should call the *wait* intrinsic, i.e., put itself to sleep until an event is *caused* when $cbc = 0$. As it happens, there is a single global (systemwide) event that is *caused* when any task is terminated. The system code responding to this *caused* event, it would appear, can employ this opportunity to wake any sleeping tasks that are waiting for their respective criticalblockcounts to become zéro.

CHAPTER 6

Software Interrupts

6.1 INTRODUCTION

To round out the B6700 facility for intertask communication, the system designers have provided a software interrupt [12, 16] capability which every (systems and applications) programmer is free to exploit as he desires. A software interrupt models a hardware interrupt in nearly every respect. Recall that a hardware interrupt was thought of and implemented as an unexpected procedure call.

In the case of a software interrupt, the signal is issued normally by another task in the task family*; the recipient (of the interrupt) will have designated and defined (in advance) the procedure that should be executed upon receipt of the interrupt signal. The recipient task is free to ignore such signals by temporarily (or permanently) disabling a software interrupt, which is in almost strict analogy with current practice of permitting the masking of hardware interrupts. If the recipient task is not actually executing at the time the software signal "arrives," the system supervisor, acting on behalf of the would-be recipient, will effectively queue the interrupt signal so that an interrupt will be triggered the next time the

---

* Tasks belonging to separate jobs can also signal one another through globally defined system events. Communication between independent tasks, however, is not treated in this book.

recipient is awarded an actual processor to run on, provided that interrupt is currently enabled.

The B6700 implementation of the software interrupt facility is a relatively simple extension of the *cause* procedure (intrinsic) that has already been described. Recall that *cause* as previously described merely placed onto the ready queue any task that is currently link-listed to a given event variable. Suppose, however, it is desired that a task should be interrupted (rather than readied) upon occurrence of a given event. In this case, the task would be programmed to execute a special (interrupt) declaration and associated statements whose effect is to associate designated procedure code with a given event variable, link-listing this task to any others which may also wish to be interrupted upon occurrence of this same event. Let the event variable we are speaking of be called *ev*. Then, when and if some other task executes a statement such as

$$cause(ev);$$

or possibly

$$cause(x);$$

where x is some formal parameter that refers to *ev*, all tasks that are queued to *ev* in the I-want-to-be-interrupted sense will be interrupted if they are now running on some processor, or will be marked for interruption when next they execute. Of course, all tasks that are queued to *ev* in the I-want-to-be-readied sense will be readied. [Note that the set of tasks queued for interruption and the set of tasks queued for readying on the same event are not necessarily disjoint sets. Note also that while two or more tasks may ask to be interrupted upon occurrence of the same event, each task is also free to specify distinct procedure code to be executed when that common event occurs.]

For example, the interrupt declaration used in B6700 Algol has the form:

interrupt ⟨name of interrupt procedure⟩; ⟨statement⟩;

Thus,

interrupt *i1*; **begin** . . . **end**;

defines the code to be executed for interrupt *i1*.

An interrupt procedure may be attached to an event variable by a statement of the form:

attach ⟨name of interrupt procedure⟩ **to** ⟨event variable⟩;

For example, the code:

> **event** *ev*;
> **interrupt** *i1*; **begin** . . . **end**;
> **attach** *i1* **to** *ev*;
> **enable** *i1*;

declares the interrupt procedure *i1*, associates it with (i.e., *attaches* it to) the event variable *ev*, and enables *i1*. Thereafter (assuming *i1* remains enabled), any time *ev* is caused, procedure *i1* will be executed as an interrupt procedure. It is possible to disable *i1* by executing the statement:

> **disable** *i1*;

The default state of *i1* is *enabled*. Of course, it is also possible to dissociate (i.e., *detach i1* from *ev* by executing

> **detach** *i1*;

after which any (other) event may be attached to *i1*.

In the next section we give an illustrative example that shows the use of software interrupts and that helps us to focus on one of the typical problems associated with them. This problem is discussed at the end of this chapter.

6.2 AN ILLUSTRATIVE EXAMPLE

The program in Figure 6.1 illustrates the use of the software interrupt feature just described, together with one use of a task variable. Task synchronizing abetted by use of the *wait* intrinsic is also illustrated. In this program, our final variant of the Figure 3.8 algorithm, the main task delegates (all) the summing of square roots to a task *t1* that executes a procedure *sumit4* (at line 8). While *t1* proceeds asynchronously, the main task busies itself with other matters (lines 29–33). The main task waits (at line 34) for completion of *t1*. Meanwhile, if *t1* runs into any trouble (negative values

```
Line
No.
  0    begin
  1      integer j, n, negcount; real total, result;
  2      array num[0 : 99]; label abort, fin;
  3      event ev1, neg, t1resume;
  4      task t1;
  5      procedure sumit4(a, s, l, sum, done, holler, resume);
  6        value s, l; integer s, l; real sum; array a[*];
  7        event done, holler, resume;
  8        begin integer i; sum ← 0;
  9          for i ← s step 1 until l do
 10            if a[i] < 0 then
 11              begin cause(holler); wait(resume);
 11a               reset(resume); sum ← 0 end
 12            else sum ← sum + sqrt(a[i]);
 13          cause(done)
 14        end sumit4
 15
 16    interrupt i1; begin
 17                    total ← total + result;
 18                    negcount ← negcount + 1;
 19                    if negcount > .05 × n
 20                        then
 21                            begin terminate(t1); go to abort end;
 22                            cause(t1resume);
 23                    end;
 24      attach i1 to neg;
 25      enable i1;
 26      negcount ← 0; total ← 0;
 27      [input the value of n and the set {num_j, for j = 0 step 1 until
            n − 1]}
 28      process sumit4(num, 0, n − 1, result, ev1, neg, t1resume) [t1];
  ⋮           ⋮  } other useful work
 34      wait(ev1);
 35      print(result, negcount, "an appropriate comment");
 36      go to fin;
 37      abort: print("negcount too high. task t1 aborted")
  ⋮           ⋮  } alternate plan
 60      fin:
 61    end
```

Figure 6.1 A program that exhibits conversational control between two tasks.

of num_i discovered at line 10), it interrupts the main task and then waits for orders from the main task in response to the interrupt. This coding is shown on line 11. The event parameter *holler* is used to *cause* the interruption of the main task via the interrupt *i1*; the parameter *resume* is an event to which task *t1* queues itself (thus moving to a wait state). If the main task is interrupted by *t1* (*i1* is always enabled in this illustration), the interrupt code checks to see if the cumulative number of negative num_i's thus far encountered by *t1* exceeds a tolerable limit (line 19). If so, the main task prepares to "throw in the towel," so to speak. It terminates task *t1* (line 21) and proceeds with an alternative strategy after first reporting the trouble (at line 37). If the number of bad values does not exceed the limit (specified in line 19), task *t1* is alerted to resume its work via the call to *cause* (at line 22). Since the call to *wait* at line 11 may occur several times, the parameter *resume* is reset to "not happened" after each return from *wait* at line 11a. After *cause*ing *t1* to resume, the main task is now allowed to continue with its own work at the point of interruption wherever that happened to be.

There are a few loose ends that remain to be discussed concerning our example. The first item is a rather minor issue which, by considering it here, allows us to further illustrate the B6700 facilities for intertasking. The second item, however, refers to a serious flaw in the Figure 6.1 program. Though we point out this flaw here, we shall defer a full discussion of ways to correct it to the end of this chapter.

1. The procedure *terminate* that is invoked on line 21 is not, as it would appear, a system intrinsic. Hence, in an actual B6700 program, *terminate* must be explicitly coded either at the point of invocation (at line 21) or in the block head of the program as a macro definition.

A possible macro definition for *terminate* might be:

```
0   define terminate(taskid) =
1     begin
2       reset(myself.exceptionevent);
3       taskid.status ← "terminated";
4       wait(myself.exceptionevent);
5     end
```

Examination of the code allows us to make two useful observations. An assignment of the code value, "terminated" to a task status attribute will receive immediate interpretation by the system. (That is, the interpretation of the new status value will not be deferred as when any other value, e.g., "suspended" is assigned to the status attribute.) For this reason, the effect of line 3 is to indeed cause termination of the target task immediately, whether the task is running, ready, or waiting on an event. If a task *A*, that is attempting to cause termination of a task *B*, wishes to halt until it receives a positive acknowledgment from the system that *B* has in fact been terminated, then code such as given on lines 2 and 4 are in order.

To understand lines 2 and 4, it should be recalled from Chapter 4 that the default value for an offspring task's exceptiontask attribute is the name of its parent. The *cause*ing of *myself.exceptionevent* will occur only at the time the system has in fact changed taskid's state to "terminated," and not before.

2. Suppose the main task has already reached and executed *wait(ev1)* on line 34, while *t1* is still executing. The main task would now be Q-threaded to *ev1*. A subsequent attempt by *t1* to interrupt the main task cannot (unfortunately) succeed simply by *cause*ing *neg* (or its dummy, *holler*) which has been attached to *i1*. In the current software implementation, *cause*ing *holler* merely instructs the system to queue the interrupt, i.e., to force the main task to execute *i1* only when next it is readied. But who will ready it? At first glance, it seems to be a simple matter to correct the program simply by inserting:

cause(done);

in *sumit4*, say immediately following *cause(holler)* on line 11. While this will certainly achieve the immediate objective of readying the main task so that it is now able to resume by executing *i1*, other, perhaps more subtle problems will then arise that must also be considered. For this reason we shall defer discussion of this matter until Section 6.4 after having taken an initial look at the B6700 data structures for software interrupts.

6.3 DATA STRUCTURES FOR SOFTWARE INTERRUPTS

In this discussion of software interrupts we shall provide the reader a glimpse into the B6700 implementation scheme itself so that, among other things, he can gain some appreciation of the processing costs that would be incurred in the use of these facilities. We mentioned earlier that an event is a structured variable whose storage structure is allocated in the activation record corresponding to the block in which the event is declared. Its structure may be viewed (in PL/1 style) as:

```
1   event
      2   happened_indicator(bit)
      2   wait_head
            3   first_waiting_task(stack no.)
            3   last_waiting_task(stack no.)
      2   interrupt_head
            3   first_task_wishing_to_be_interrupted(stack no.)
            3   last_task_wishing_to_be_interrupted(stack no.)
```

In effect, an event is a header for two doubly linked lists or queues of tasks, each designated by its stack number. (Stack numbers are discussed in Chapter 9.) Tasks may appear on both lists. The first list (call it the *event wait queue*) designates the tasks that want to be readied when the happened indicator of the event is turned on. The second list (call it the *event interrupt queue*) designates the tasks that want to be interrupted when the happened indicator is turned on.

We need say no more here about the event wait queue. Each entry in the event interrupt queue appears in the activation record of the procedure declaring that interrupt. Thus, if the declaration

interrupt x; ⟨interrupt procedure⟩;

appears in a procedure named y, then in the activation record y' there is a compiler-generated, computer-allocated interrupt queue entry. In essence, this entry consists of a queue linkage word, a pointer to the interrupt procedure, and a bit to indicate if this interrupt is presently enabled. [Use of the interrupt queue linkage word makes it possible to queue a task for interrupt while the same task may be queued (through its Q-thread) on a wait or ready queue.] When *cause* works its way through the entries of the event interrupt queue, it does the following for each enabled entry that is encountered.

Let the interrupt queue entry we are speaking of be found in the stack for task *t*. Then the pointer to the interrupt procedure code is threaded onto a special one-per-task "software interrupt queue" whose list header is found in task *t*'s task information area (that area of each stack below the first activation record that is set aside by the system for its own use). If the task involved now happens to be executing on one of the system's processors, *cause* sees to it that a special hardware interrupt is generated. This forces the processor to execute an interrupt handling routine that will execute the procedure whose pointer was just threaded on task *t*'s software interrupt queue. Upon completion of this interrupt procedure, control will return to the point of interruption (which may well be inside another interrupt procedure).

If task *t* is not running on an actual processor at the time *cause* adds the interrupt procedure pointer to task *t*'s software interrupt queue, then no further action with respect to task *t* is taken.* Instead, *cause* "moves on" to do the same chore for the next entry on the event interrupt queue. Task *t* will get its turn to run on a processor if and only if the event for which it is wait-queued is *caused*. When this happens, the very first code executed by task *t* will be to see if its software interrupt queue is empty. If it is not empty, then, assuming the interrupt procedures execute returns, each interrupt procedure whose pointer is found in the queue is then executed. When all such procedures have been executed, control is returned to the point where the task would ordinarily have resumed had no interrupts accumulated during the period of suspension.

Figures 6.2 and 6.3 show two self-explained execution snapshots of the Figure 6.1 algorithm. These snapshots illustrate the various queue threadings that we have just described.

---

* This is because it is not permissible to force task *t* into the ready list and give it a processor so that the interrupt procedure can be executed. Such a practice, if permitted, would lead to other complications, as discussed in Section 6.4.

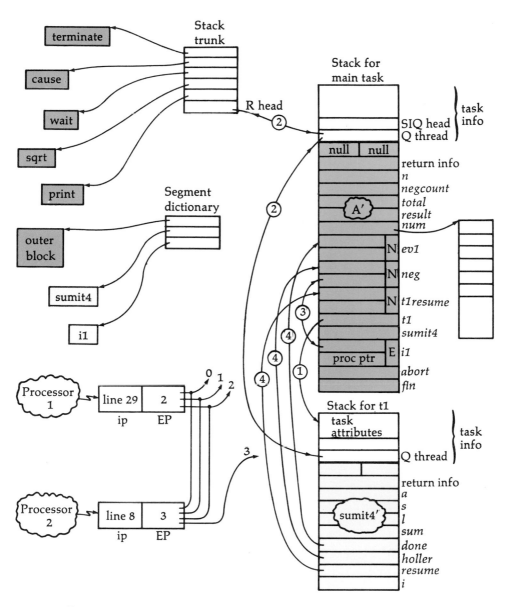

Figure 6.2 Snapshot of the Figure 6.1 algorithm when task *t1* starts execution and the main task is executing (asynchronously) at line 29. The line marked ① shows the main task's pointer to task *t1*'s task attributes. The lines marked ② show the ready queue. The line marked ③ shows how interrupt *i1* is queued (in the event interrupt sense) to *neg*. The part of *i1* marked "proc ptr" points to the code block *i1*. The lines marked ④ remind us that formal event parameters, *done, holler*, and *resume* are called by reference. Events *ev1*, *neg* and *t1resume* are not happened (N). Interrupt *i1* is enabled (E).

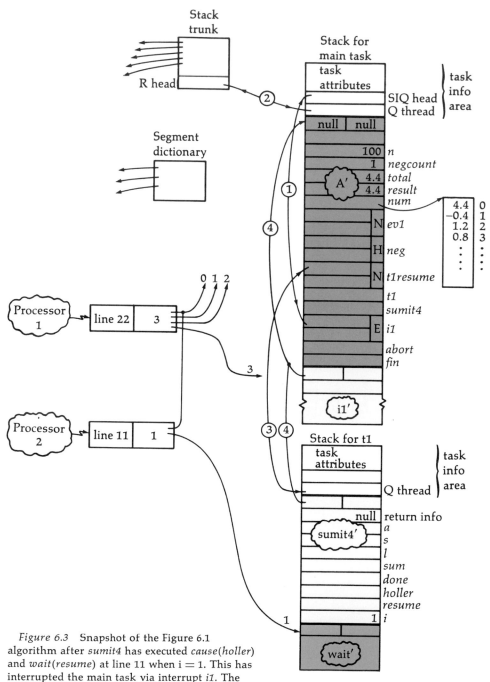

Figure 6.3 Snapshot of the Figure 6.1
algorithm after *sumit4* has executed *cause(holler)*
and *wait(resume)* at line 11 when i = 1. This has
interrupted the main task via interrupt *i1*. The
main task is now pictured as just about to execute line 22. The line marked ① suggests the
software interrupt queue (SIQ) threading. (However, this SIQ thread is actually cut just prior
to executing the procedure *i1*.) Line ② is the ready thread. Line ③ shows *t1* event-wait queued
to *t1resume*. Lines ④ are static links.

Procedure pointers for disabled interrupts are carried in the software interrupt queue along with those for enabled interrupts but are not acted on by the interrupt handler. However, if, after a disabled interrupt has been *caused*, the interrupt is re-enabled, then a proper adjustment is made to the corresponding entry in the software interrupt queue. In essence, therefore, a software interrupt "signal" that arrives when an interrupt has been disabled is remembered and acted on when the interrupt has been re-enabled.

6.4 INTERRUPTING A SLEEPING TASK AND OTHER PROBLEMS

We are now ready to resume our discussion of the flaw in the program displayed in Figure 6.1. That program failed to make provision for awakening the "sleeping" main task, so it could execute the interrupt procedure *il* and then, in this case, make it go back to sleep again (at the old wait point). In general, if we manage to awaken a task so that it can respond to an interrupt, what or how can we prevent it from forgetting that it had been asleep and that it should now go back to sleep for the same old reason? Technically, this difficulty arises because an interrupt procedure is designed to effect a normal return to the instruction that would be executed next had the interrupt not occurred. Unfortunately, for the case of a sleeping task that had been interrupted, this next instruction is not a repeat of the call on *wait* but rather the return point from the call on *wait*. Thus, if we manage to awaken the task that should be interrupted, by synthetically *cause*ing the waited-for event, then upon return from the interrupt procedure, control will skip right past the wait point and continue on as if the waited-for event had really happened. Such a practice is guaranteed to cause a catastrophe in most instances unless some suitable coding is provided as a "preventative."

The most straightforward approach toward solving the problem just described takes advantage of the so-called "complex wait" function, a B6700 variant of the *wait* intrinsic. The complex wait has as arguments, a *list* of event identifiers rather than a single one. The function returns an integer whose value represents the position in the "wait list" of the argument that has been *caused*.

The use of the complex wait is now illustrated. Suppose line 34 of Figure 6.1 were replaced by:

$$\textbf{while } wait(ev1, neg) = 2 \textbf{ do};$$

The wait *function* performs all those actions described above for the *wait* intrinsic. Additionally, it returns a value; in the example, the value is:

      1   if *ev1* has happened
      2   if *neg* but not *ev1* has happened

If *ev1* is the first of the two events to be *caused*, the interpretation is that the offspring task has successfully completed its work. Since the complex wait function will then return a value of 1, the **while** clause will be evaluated as **false**, and execution continues to lines 35, etc. However, if *neg* is the first event to be *caused*, the main task will be readied and then "trapped" to the interrupt routine *i1*. This is because the main task is now not only threaded on to the event interrupt queue, but also on to the event wait queue for *neg*. Upon normal return from *i1*, a wait function value of 2 will be returned (at line 34), resulting in a **true** value for the **while** clause. Since the statement to be executed by the **do** is null, the net effect is that evaluation of the **while** clause is repeated. Hence the main task cannot proceed to line 35 until *ev1* has been *caused*; during its hold at line 34, however, it can be interrupted by any number of interrupts such as *i1*, and all such interrupts will be handled correctly.

It is now easy to see why *i1* must be modified so that it remains responsive to repeated interrupt attempts. This may be accomplished by rewriting line 16 as:

$$\textbf{interrupt } i1; \textbf{ begin } reset(neg);$$

To summarize, an appeal to the complex wait allows us to clear up the difficulty of interrupting a sleeping task in a fairly nice way. The author has found alternative solutions to this problem that do not require the use of a complex wait intrinsic, but these solutions were rather awkward at best.

It is reassuring to know, when invoking the complex wait intrinsic in more general applications, that this function has been implemented with interlocks which guarantee that one and only one event argument on the wait list can effectively cause the awakening of a task. This prevents confusion in identifying which of several waited-for events is to "get credit for" awakening the sleeping task. Of course in the particular case we chose to illustrate, there can be no confusion, since the origin of events *ev1* and *neg* are mutually exclusive.

6.5 RESOURCE-ORIENTED SYNCHRONIZING PRIMITIVES

Readers who have found the foregoing study of interest will want to investigate some of the other task synchronizing intrinsics that are offered in the B6700 software (which are detailed in the reference literature). Not the least among these is the pair of "resource-oriented" functions, *procure* and *liberate*. These allow a task to enter and exit from what Dijkstra calls a "critical section" of a program. These intrinsics, and several variants of them, function as locking and unlocking primitives by taking advantage of a second property of an event which so far has gone unmentioned. Previously we regarded the event as being in essence a bistable, either *happened* or *not happened*. In the actual B6700 implementation, each event has a second property bit which has the resource-oriented, two-state interpretation *available* and *not available*. A task that executes a statement of the form

procure(ev);

is forced into the wait state if the event *ev* is not available, but otherwise is allowed to execute the next statement in sequence. Thus a critical section coded in Burroughs Algol takes the form:

procure(ev);

—

—

—

—

liberate(ev);

6.6 SOFTWARE INTERRUPT CAVEATS

Although a good deal of emphasis has been given to the concept and implementation of the software interrupt, two caveats are in order.

1. It should be clear that the implementation mechanisms for software interrupt involve more overhead than the simpler event queuing (*wait* and *cause*) forms of task synchronizing. Effective use of the complex wait function, as we gain more experience with it, may make it possible to achieve effects similar to those obtainable with the software interrupt, with less execution overhead in many cases. The tradeoff, where a choice is available, appears to be clarity of the program's semantics (on the side of the software interrupts) versus efficiency (on the side of the "simpler" event queuing mechanisms).

2. Other pitfalls associated with the use of software interrupts quite apart from the one just discussed have been observed by implementers of this type of software. For example, the interrupted procedure or its dynamic antecedent may have been a system intrinsic which has just locked a key data base. The interrupt procedure may prevent return to the interrupted procedure (or to its antecedent) so as to unlock that data base or otherwise restore certain key system data to a "consistent" state. Unsolved problems remain in this area and a full discussion of this topic is beyond the scope of this book.

CHAPTER 7

On Storage Control Strategies

7.1 STORAGE CONTROL AT BLOCK EXIT

As mentioned in Chapter 5, deallocation is close-coupled with program- or procedure-block exit in the current B6700 implementation. This implies a discipline for recovery of all no-longer-needed storage resources and explicit adjustment to prevent "dangling pointers." A dangling pointer is any reference to an information object (i.e., an array, an I/O buffer area, an activation record, etc.) that has been deleted from the address space of the computation. This type of resource management is done at block exit time and is the responsibility of system routines, calls to which are generated by the compilers at block exit and procedure return points in the algorithm.

The routine *blockexit*, calls to which are generated when needed, checks among other things for the presence of arrays that have been allocated outside the stack (e.g., the *num* array in the Figure 3.8 program) during the current instance of execution (activation) of the block being exited (e.g., A), and returns all such array space either to the proper free storage pool or to disk file storage.

If an activation record that is being deallocated contains one (or more) interrupt queue entries, then one (or more) such interrupt queue chains would be severed leaving dangling pointers, possibly in this stack (when deallocating a software interrupt queue entry), or in *other* stacks (when deallocating an event interrupt queue entry). The *blockexit* system routine does the needed repair work to all the affected queue links that are connected to those in the block being deallocated, and this action prevents the introduction of dangling pointers.

The design philosophy employed in implementing these resource management functions has the desirable characteristic that a user's program will evoke (i.e., "pay for") only those services which his own program actually requires. The remainder of this section explains why. One may note that what is said here concerning block-structured Algol program also applies to programs written in Basic, Fortran, etc., which can be regarded as degenerate cases of Algol programs.

As a block is compiled, the compiler maintains information regarding the characteristics of the local addressing space. If only stack space is to be used, i.e., the "locals" are all simple variables, then the code generated for the **end** statement is simply Exit (a single B6700 instruction). If arrays, files, interrupts, etc., are declared in the block, then a call to the routine *blockexit* must be generated for the **end** statement. In the latter event, the compiler generates an auxiliary variable which, during execution of the entry to the block being compiled, is placed in the activation record on top of the cells for the declared locals. This auxiliary variable is a special "Software Control Word," the bit pattern of which is interpreted by *blockexit*. Thus, one particular bit means local arrays exist, another means that file close action may be required due to local files, etc. We see that *blockexit* is called only if necessary and, when called, is "told" precisely what functions it must perform, so essentially no superfluous activity is ever undertaken.

7.2 PREVENTING DANGLING POINTERS

It is worth observing that as the richness of our programming language increases, and as programmers learn to exploit such richness, the potential (occasions) for dangling pointers will inevitably increase. Moreover, short of developing compensating hardware improvements or going to alternative software implementation schemes, it can be appreciated that the overhead costs associated

Line
No.

1	**begin ref int** p;	¢ p is declared to be a pointer to an integer ¢
2	**begin int** $i := 1$;	¢ i is declared and initialized to 1 ¢
3	$p := i$	¢ p is made to point to i ¢
4	**end**	¢ block in which i is declared is exited ¢
5	$print(p)$	¢ depending on the deallocation strategy, this printing ¢
6	**end**	¢ of value pointed to by p will not or will work ¢

Figure 7.1 An Algol 68 program [5] to illustrate the dangling pointer problem.

with preventing the dangling pointer are bound to increase. Languages like Euler, Algol 68, and PL/1 may be cited to illustrate this concern. Such languages allow the use of procedure and label variables (in addition to procedure and label constants). In PL/1 we also see permitted not only the use of variables of type pointer, but also the use of *allocate* and *free* statements, thereby introducing an increased hazard of dangling pointers [58].

Assigning a value to a procedure or label variable amounts to assigning (ip, ep) pairs to such variables. Let X be the variable to which such a value is assigned. If the "lifetime" of X exceeds that of the data object(s) Y referenced by the ep of the (ip, ep) pair, then the potential for a dangling pointer arises when Y is deallocated (before X).

For programs written in block-structured languages, the concept of lifetime can, at some risk of oversimplification, be informally defined as follows: The variable X would have a lifetime exceeding that of Y if the activation record containing the cell for Y were deallocated via block exit before deallocation of the record containing the cell for X.

Figure 7.1 is an example of a simple Algol 68 program used by Berry [5] to highlight the dangling pointer problem. Comments contained in the illustration help to make the program self-explanatory to those unfamiliar with Algol 68. The last remark in the comments will be explained momentarily.

Several recent studies [5, 37, 58] have reviewed approaches to preventing dangling pointers. Two ways to achieve this objective are:

1. Place constraints on the semantics of the programming language so that

    (a) the compiler intervenes to reject any assignment statement whose effect would be to assign a reference to an object that has a lifetime shorter than the cell to which the assignment is to be made; or

    (b) the run-time (interpreter) routines somehow invalidate such assignment steps when attempt is made to execute them.

2. Decouple the deallocation of activation records (and of other associated information objects) from the block exit activity of a computation. *Retain* such information as long as there exist (in the rest of the record of execution) pointers to such information. An information object then becomes a candidate for deallocation (i.e., for recovery in the resource management sense) only when there are no longer any pointer variables whose values point to the candidate.

Several investigations have reviewed the arguments to support the second approach [5, 6, 37, 58]. The reader's attention is called to this literature for a deeper study. Implementation of scheme 1 employs a *deletion discipline* that is facilitated with the use of stacks as described in this monograph. For implementation of scheme 2, however, which uses a *retention discipline*, stacks as we now know them are not likely to prove useful enough. We can speculate that some hardware improvements that would make for efficient link-listing of activation records [52] might help, though perhaps not enough. Rather different hardware approaches [37] may prove necessary. We can look forward to some interesting developments in hardware organization over the next decade, some of which may be aimed at solving the dangling pointers problem via a retention discipline.

Returning to the consideration of the Figure 7.1 program, we can now note that if the deletion discipline (or strategy) is followed, the cell for i must of course be deallocated at exit from the inner block. The responsibility may be left to the *blockexit* routine to find any and all pointers to objects in the deallocated record. In this case, the pointer p would be found and its value invalidated. As a consequence the statement on line 5,

$$print(p)$$

will fail, e.g., will cause an error return. We might picture this approach as a direct extension of the current B6700 implementation philosophy.

If on the other hand, retention is assumed, the activation record containing the cell for i is retained at the time of exit from the inner block because one cell in it is still accessible from p. As a result the pointer p remains valid and the $print(p)$ statement will be successfully executed. Thus, this example suggests that though both storage management strategies are implementable, they cannot be expected to yield identical results in all instances.

CHAPTER 8

The B6700: Pros and Cons

8.1 INTRODUCTION

In much of the preceding text the author has described the B6700 organization structure and its "matching" software from the point of view of an enthusiastic admirer of its design and of the philosophy that underlies it. To gain some extra perspective, this chapter attempts to review and comment on several oft-mentioned alleged weaknesses of the present system. Other limitations and the possible system modifications that can remove such limitations are also discussed.

Systems are often criticized or appraised from three viewpoints: That of the languages available to users and the cost effectiveness of user programs; that of the operating system and what it lets the user do (or not do); and that of the hardware. It is not always easy to separate these interrelated system capabilities in a discussion on the limitations of the B6700. The remainder of this chapter is nevertheless structured with these three major viewpoints in mind.

8.2 USER LANGUAGES AND USER PROGRAM PERFORMANCE

The difficulty in attempting to separate language, from operating system and hardware is especially evident when trying to analyze why it is widely conceded that B6700 programs written in Fortran do not as a rule execute as fast as comparable Fortran programs execute on less structured computer systems [e.g., on von Neumann machines that use index registers and/or base registers (but not stack-based descriptors) for data accessing] of comparable arithmetic and memory speeds. There exists, of course, the companion observation that is also worth examining at the same time; namely, many B6700 algorithms for numerical computations execute more efficiently (in time and space) when coded as Algol-like programs than when coded as Fortran programs. (The latter phenomenon may not surprise us since the B6700-type system was designed with the specific intention of facilitating the execution of Algol-like programs.) Be that as it may, since most computer installations must run some Fortran programs, and some computer installations run mostly Fortran programs, it is important to understand the underlying language and interrelated operating system and hardware considerations that together may explain these performance differences.

The highly structured B6700 differs from typical machines in both instruction fetch and data accessing costs. On the plus side, fewer memory cycles are typically required for fetching B6700 instructions, and on the minus side, more memory cycles are required for accessing data. Barton [2] has pointed out that, given an Algol-like execution environment, these plus and minus factors roughly cancel one another and what is left is the residual advantage for the B6700 type machine, namely, that the code body for the B6700 algorithm is significantly smaller (occupies less memory), and that all data accessing carries with it as a bonus, (a) the benefit of having to allocate primary memory space only for those substructures of data aggregates that are actually needed and (b) the assurance of full protection against bounds errors and other access violations (deliberate or accidental).

The explanation is as follows: Variable-length B6700 instructions frequently have no address fields at all since the operand location(s) is (are) implied to be in some specific spot(s) at or near the top of the stack. This means that B6700 instructions are on the average shorter than their counterparts in von Neumann-type machines. The shorter B6700 instructions, called "syllables," are packed several per word, hence each memory cycle taken for an instruction fetch usually retrieves more instructions than an instruction fetch on a competitive conventional machine.

On the other hand, data accessing for items outside the stack requires that at least one descriptor be brought to the top of the stack and employed as an indirect (base) address. Thus at least one extra memory cycle is often unavoidable for fetching array elements. There are no fast registers whose use is dedicated for holding descriptors as in most large conventional machines. When a data structure element has several defining indices, a descriptor must be fetched for each index, unless the multidimensional array has been "linearized." This means, for example, that as the frequency and degree of array indexing increases, the execution cost balance mentioned earlier tips to the negative side. That is, programs tend to become more costly to execute on the present B6700 than on systems that employ dedicated base address and/or index registers. It is for this reason that the B6700 designers have often argued against recommending their highly structured machine for installations in which the dominant application is claimed to consist of numerical computation on arrays (e.g., large matrix inversions).

On the other hand, the use of "dope-vectors" of descriptors for the structuring of data aggregates offers an important tradeoff to offset the extra accessing cost just mentioned. Not only is it unnecessary to commit memory space for substructures, e.g., rows of an array, until actually needed, but each such substructure is individually overlayable. This may result in savings in space which of course means savings in time. One must also bear in mind important tradeoffs that obtain in this case between execution speeds and protection. A highly structured machine like the B6700 requires data accessing through system-constructed descriptors. This "constraint" offers built-in protection benefits by preventing a large class of run-time accessing errors and illegal access attempts. Users are protected both from others and from themselves. The significance of the protection issue cannot be minimized [19, 28, 40, 46], although we have arbitrarily excluded a full discussion of the issue in this text. Appeal to the tradeoff issue of protection is not to say however that the B6700 hardware structure cannot or will not evolve toward speedier data accessing. The technical feasibility of this advancement is discussed further in Section 8.4.

We are now ready to see why ASA Standard Fortran programs may execute slower than corresponding Algol-like programs on the B6700. The semantics of the Fortran EQUIVALENCE and COMMON declarations are such that use of these declarations effectively forces a compiler to allocate contiguous blocks of storage for arrays that fall under the purview of these declarations.* Algol-like languages do not allow such declarations; hence all structured variables (e.g., arrays) in such languages are memorywise independent. Moreover, components of structures, e.g., rows of arrays, can be allocated to separate and relocatable memory areas (each pointed to by an appropriate descriptor).

There are two costs associated with this Fortran constraint:

1. Finding a contiguous block of memory that is large enough to serve. (This is a memory management problem.) The allocation cost perhaps depends as much on the allocation strategies that are chosen as on the hardware organization of the system. This cost, which increases with the size of the block needed, could well be comparable on machines of widely different organization structure.

2. Achieving data access to individual array elements. This cost depends on the degree of indexing required and/or on the organization of the hardware. On machines that employ indexing hardware, the compiled code need not suffer in efficiency, but for a B6700-type structure, part of the address must be computed arithmetically at run time from the base address given by the descriptor for the entire region. Thus, the effective index for $A_{i,j}$ involves a run-time evaluation of the expression: $(j - 1) \times imax + i - 1$. The greater degree of indexing, the greater will be the number of instructions required to compute the desired offset into the memory block. This computational overhead is in addition to that incurred by the descriptor mechanism. Worse yet, none of the tradeoff advantages associated with the descriptor accrue in this instance.

* Perhaps another way of stating this is that Fortran was designed for a fixed-address machine (the IBM 704).

We see therefore that the second cost cited is the chief source of the penalty for executing B6700 programs written in ASA Fortran. Observation: If one were content to write Fortran programs which were "equivalence free," so to speak, then it would be an easy matter to adjust the compiler to allocate array space in independent blocks, one per each structured variable or structured component thereof. Doing this would put Fortran programs that make heavy use of arrays on par with comparable Algol programs when executed on a system like the B6700. Insisting on equivalence-free Fortran programs is a matter of style in the same sense as Dijkstra's now widely accepted insistence on avoiding the **go to** statement in Algol programs by a judicious substitution of conditionals, procedure calls, and **for** statements. In any case one could well ask, "What price, Fortran?"

Other language and operating system considerations are often discussed in connection with the B6700-type system. For instance, one may wonder why it is that relatively so few language processors were in use by "customers" of the B5700 series—although this system was widely used for many years. (It is too early to make a comparable observation for the B6700.) Is there something about the structure of the machine or of the operating system that made compilers for the B5700 hard to implement? Several explanations can be offered to suggest that this was not the case, and indeed, that quite the opposite is more likely to be true.

1. The manufacturer chose to commit only a seemingly skeletal force for the software support effort. This proved feasible because of the strong coupling of two important factors: (a) the system's architecture which caters for execution of Algol-like programs and (b) the decision to write *all* software in Algol-like languages.

2. Customers were typically content to use the equipment with the supplied language processors. They were rarely motivated to appreciate the unusual structure and design philosophy of the supporting hardware and operating system. (It must be said that the B5700 series had many commercial and few academic customers.) We, of course, bear in mind

that a compiler for any advanced system must produce code that fits into the system's special operating environment, e.g., multiprogramming, multiprocessing, protected addressing, etc., and that insures correct communication with the system-supplied intrinsics. A customer who failed to "do his homework" would therefore not be likely to produce his own specially-tailored language processor.

3. Customers soon learned that the Algol-like compilers offered by the manufacturer amounted to a language hierarchy that permitted a programmer to express rather easily a wide range of information processing operations from the most machine-independent levels to the most detailed machine-dependent descriptions. Exemplified in B6700 terms, this hierarchy of high-level language processors [41] now includes three principal components: namely, Extended Algol, DC Algol [9] (an outgrowth of a special data communications language), and Espol [11]. Programs can be constructed by binding segments that are separately compiled by each of these processors. Availability of Espol to the user eliminates his need for an assembly language processor. Availability of the rich Algol tends to reduce and often eliminate the user's need for special purpose higher level languages, e.g., for string or list processing. Availability of DC Algol encourages a subsystem designer to develop his own suboperating system. Moreover, macroprocessors written in Algol may be easily constructed to produce translators from given special purpose languages to one of the languages in the above "triplet."

4. Intrinsics and easily modifiable compilers allow one to tailor a compiler to one's needs without going to a new language.

5. Users of the B6700 system may bind Cobol, Fortran, Algol, and DC Algol code segments into single programs.

The first of our foregoing "explanations" suggests an important observation; namely, a system that has been designed to facilitate development of its software in high-level languages and whose supporting software is made easier to understand because it too has been coded in high-level language is one for which new software is easier to produce than for systems in which coding in low-level languages is encouraged. Ten years ago [1961] this Burroughs approach was unique. More recently, at least one other major system (Multics [46]) has been implemented with this philosophy. The idea has gained an increasing number of adherents, but so far no other manufacturer has marketed such a system on a commercial basis.

8.3 THE OPERATING SYSTEM

One has to go out of one's way to find many serious shortcomings in the B6700 operating system. Two that are frequently discussed among designers and builders of the system's software will be mentioned in the following subsections.

8.3.1 Richer Set of Synchronizing and Software Interrupt Primitives

Multitasking as a user facility is still quite new. Formalizing of primitives for use in communication among cooperating sequential tasks [26, 27] is only now coming of age. Even though the B6700 operating system is one of the first to fully cater to this approach to programming, one suspects that much still has to be learned about the subject. The discussion of the program in Figure 6.4 (how to interrupt a sleeping task and what system software/hardware is needed) was a case in point. Should one provide for passing parameters to interrupt procedures? What other primitives besides *wait* and *cause* should be provided as alternatives (e.g., semaphores P and V [27], critical regions [29] and conditional critical regions [33], facilities for wakeup with a message included [56], etc.)?

8.3.2. Recursively Defined Resource Allocation

Although a primary goal of the B6700 hardware and software is to cater to recursion in programming at all levels, it can be argued that the development can still go further, perhaps with further benefits. Is the operating system itself recursively defined? That is, can a sequence of operating systems be developed by users that function under the system's own master control program? In particular, is space (and other resource) allocation recursively defined for potential exploitation by users? The answer is no, not in any fully general sense. Readers may wish to study this question further [30].

8.4 HARDWARE LIMITATIONS AND FUTURE IMPROVEMENTS

In comparing the B6700-type of system with conventional systems that are thought to be of "advanced" design, some readers may wonder what, if any, disadvantages have been introduced by the B5700/B6700 design choice to favor hardware segmentation while rejecting hardware paging mechanisms that do not reflect the information structure of the program. The pros and cons of this issue have unfortunately not been widely understood, although the excellent discussion by Randell and Kuehner [49] on dynamic storage allocation systems should go a long way toward explaining the tradeoffs that are involved. In essence, a design that favors allocation of variable-sized segments saves storage space at the expense of added processing time to locate space of suitable size while a design that favors allocation of memory in fixed-sized page blocks saves processing time (to find a unit of storage allocation) at the expense of wasted space, i.e., "internal fragmentation," which arises whenever the space required does not exactly utilize an integral number of page blocks. The time overheads associated with searching for the right segment size and returning the portion left over to the free list (and maintaining the lists) can be minimized with suitable hardware, and some of this (although perhaps not enough) has already been accomplished in the B6700 system. There is not very much that can be done in hardware to offset the space wastage of the paging approach, although some attempts have been made to produce machines that permit page blocks to be variable in size [43].

In Section 8.3.2, we discussed among other things the desirability of a hierarchy of operating systems (MCP's).* Allied with this is

---

* Burroughs has referred, for years, to its operating systems as Master Control Programs, or MCP's.

the concept of a hierarchy of storage control. Thus a task could hand control to another task and at the same time hand over a block of storage to that descendent task. This is precisely the case with the current MCP and "everything else," but there are only two levels of storage control and the desire is for multilevels—in fact, as many levels of storage control as there are levels in the task tree. It is difficult to overemphasize the advantages of such an approach.

In Section 8.3.2 we also pointed out that such a storage control strategy has not been achieved on the B6700. It could, however, not even be *considered* if a paging rather than a segmentation mechanism had been implemented. (The reader is urged to convince himself of this.) With the segmentation approach, there is still potential for development in such a direction, and it could well be that such development would constitute the major advantage of the segmentation approach.

In Section 8.2 we noted that the current hardware often puts the B6700 at some disadvantage for executing programs that involve a great deal of indexing. Barton [3] has asserted that an adequately large "fast stack top," i.e., a sufficient number of words, say 32, at the top of the stack that are composed of fast registers, provides the solution to the above problem.* By increasing the stack top and without altering the instruction repertoire, the key descriptors can be brought to the stack top by the normal procedure call and kept there during the course of the program loops in which fast access to them is required. Other schemes which have the same net effect may be developed. Barton has also suggested that the enlarged fast-stack-top approach has the further virtue of offering a convenient opportunity to introduce hardware-supported vector operations, and in this way accomplish accessing functions which, in other systems, would be done with index registers. Hardware implementation of vector operations on a stack machine would certainly remove the residual competitive disadvantages machines like the B6700 now "suffer" in the area of array processing.

Three other areas where improvements in the hardware could well lead to overall system improvement are:

---

* Top of the stack registers, as currently implemented on the B6700, are discussed, but only briefly, in Chapter 9. See for instance, Figure 9.6.

1. Enriching (extending) the self-describing tags * for data and control words so that more hardware recognition can be effected. For instance, events are control words that are not now recognizable as such by the hardware.

2. Adding operators to perform processing on queue data structures. Since so much multitasking control depends on operations on queues, it would appear that special operators could be devised to facilitate operations on these rather standard data structures.

3. Altering the interrupt hardware so that the operating system can increase its control over which processor may recognize interrupts by source and by type.

All of these observations of possible hardware improvement, and several more, are recognized by the system's designers and implementers. Readers of this monograph who become interested in the issues mentioned will find study in this area to be stimulating and rewarding.

In summary, the language, software, and hardware limitations that were just discussed seem mainly to point to potential improvements in the system that can minimize or remove these limitations. There appear to be no blunders, although when the initial B5000 system was first introduced it was so little understood that many were convinced otherwise. It is hoped that the approach taken in this book has provided a useful basis for appreciating these remarkable systems, which in many respects have been ahead of their time.

* Tag details on the B6700 are described in Chapter 9. See Figure 9.2.

Some Hardware Details of Procedure Entry and Return and Tasking

by J. G. CLEARY*

9.1 OVERVIEW

Much of the power of the B6700 hardware and software lies in the uniform treatment that has been given to procedure calls, interrupts and task calls. In Chapters 2–7 we tried to keep the discourse at a somewhat stylistic level, avoiding many of the actual details, hoping thereby to more easily focus on the structure of computations and on the objectives of the hardware and software operations for matching and facilitating such structures. In this chapter we shall describe the B6700 hardware in greater detail than was given earlier for the benefit of the reader who has gained a sufficiently healthy curiosity. Still, the new description must be regarded as somewhat of an abstraction of the real hardware's structure and function. This is unavoidable if the details provided are to remain above the level of frequent change. It is to be hoped that readers will find that this intermediate level of description can serve as a suitable bridge to the details that are normally found in the reference manuals.

Figure 9.1 shows a view of the B6700 system while two jobs (A and B) are currently in operation. [Figures in this chapter show

* The Burroughs Corporation, England.

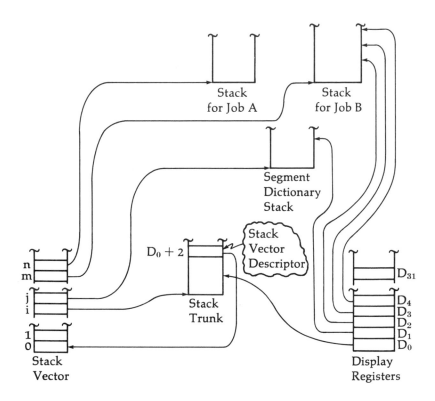

Figure 9.1   B6700 System Data Structure with two re-entrant jobs in operation. Job B is currently active [running on the (single) processing unit].

the stacks as filling from bottom to top. With this style, the terms "top of stack" or "bottom of stack" indeed refer on the diagram of a stack to top and bottom, respectively. Readers can expect to see this style used in other literature on the B6700 [8, 13, 16, 32; Appendix to 47, 48]. (The style used in Chapters 2–7, the reverse of the one used here, is actually rather unconventional.) In the figures which follow only the EP (Display Registers) of the hardware processor is shown. Registers holding the instruction pointer are omitted.

Figure 9.1 reminds us that in a single-processor system a switch of control from one job, B, to another job, A, will require resetting of Display Registers [32, 50] D_2, D_3, and D_4 and frequently, also D_1 (when separate segment dictionary stacks are used).

The initiation of a new job or task will, in general, also require resetting of Display Registers. This mechanism will be described below, but it is worth pointing out that "Display Update" is associated essentially with procedure entry and exit and that job or task initiation and termination are merely special cases of procedure entry and exit [16].

9.2 THE STACK VECTOR

All references to stacks are through Stack Numbers. The Stack Number of a stack is the ordinal of a Descriptor (see Section 9.3), within the Stack Vector, which contains the absolute address of the beginning of the memory space occupied by the stack. The Descriptor for the Stack Vector itself is contained within the Stack Trunk (see Figure 9.1) and is always at relative memory location $D_0 + 2$—i.e., two spaces above the place where the zeroth Display Register points. Hence, instructions (called "operators" on the B6700) may reference stacks indirectly via Stack Numbers. Stacks are therefore dynamically relocatable.

Since a Stack Number uniquely identifies a stack, it also uniquely identifies a job or task within a job. Though a job may be given one or more names, ultimately all such names map to the Stack Number for its representative stack. Since the Stack Vector and Stack Number are known to the computer hardware, much of the housekeeping associated with job handling is taken care of directly by hardware.

The Stack Vector may therefore be thought of as a "Job Vector." It is ultimately a list of cells which collectively point to the address space owned by each job. Since all resources owned by a job are either contained within or are referenced within its associated stack or stacks, the ownership of all resources within the system is ascertainable from the Stack Vector.

9.3 INFORMATION AND ADDRESSING STRUCTURE

Figure 9.2 shows the possible formats of the 51-bit words. The 3-bit tag field specifies the kind of information contained within

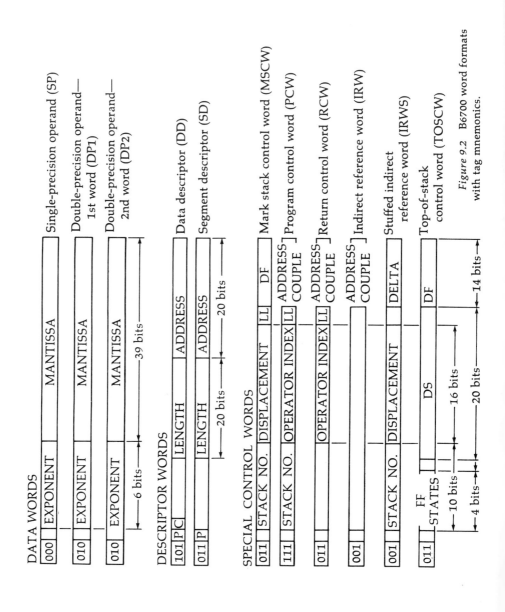

Figure 9.2   B6700 word formats with tag mnemonics.

the word, and the other 48 bits contain the actual information. Operators (instructions) treat the words according to their tagged nature. Thus single precision and double precision information is so tagged and there is no need for special single and double precision operators. For example, there is only one Add Operator which sums the two top operands in the stack and replaces them by the (one) result. The Add Operator will take any combination of double and single precision operands, integer or floating point, and will produce the appropriate—single or double precision—result. All necessary precision transformations will be handled by the hardware. (No unique integer data type exists. An integer has a zero exponent.)

Certain operators require certain word types as operands. Thus a fault interrupt will be generated if one of the operands for an Add Operator is a Control Word. Similarly, a fault interrupt will be generated if certain operators access other than Control Words.

Descriptors point at arrays of information. The information may be data (Data Descriptors) or program code (Segment Descriptors). The address field contains the absolute address of the array either in core (P field = 1) or on the disk (P field = 0). By way of review, if an attempt is made to access information, via a Descriptor, having a Presence Bit (P field) of zero, a Presence Bit Interrupt is generated and a system procedure will cause the relevant information to be moved from disk to core with appropriate modification of the Descriptor. Thus automatic "paging on demand" is catered to. (Note however that variable length segments rather than pages are the units transferred.) Any attempt to index information outside the units specified by the length field of the Descriptor will cause an Invalid Index interrupt. Data Descriptors may point to arrays of Data Descriptors thus allowing for arrays of any dimension. [Note: The use of the "C" or "copy bit" field shown in the Data Descriptor format on Figure 9.2 is explained in Section 9.4 in a discussion of Figure 9.7.]

Information may also be accessed via the (normal or stuffed) Indirect Reference Word. The Normal Indirect Reference Word (IRW) specifies (in its Address Couple field) a Display Register and a Displacement. Thus information global or local to the particular active procedure may be accessed. For example, when Job B is active, IRW's having the address couples (0, 3), (1, 4), and (2, 5)

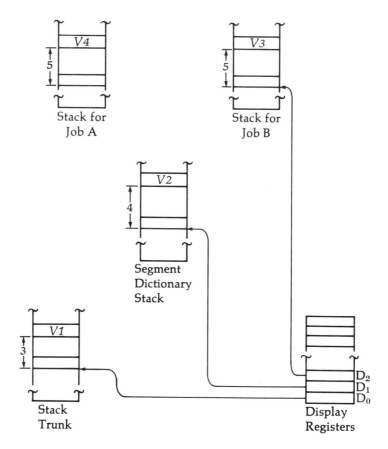

Figure 9.3 Simple Stack Tree showing addressing through Display Registers. *V1* is at (0, 3); *V2* is at (1, 4); *V3* is at (2, 5); *V4* is at (2, 5) when job A is active.

will access, respectively, in Figure 9.3: the system variable *V1* in the Stack Trunk, the job variable *V2* in the Segment Dictionary, and the global variable *V3* in Job B's stack. It should be noted that when Job A is active, Display Register settings will change and the address couple (2, 5) will then access variable *V4*.

The Stuffed Indirect Reference Word (IRWS) specifies three things: (a) a Stack Number and thus a particular stack, (b) the

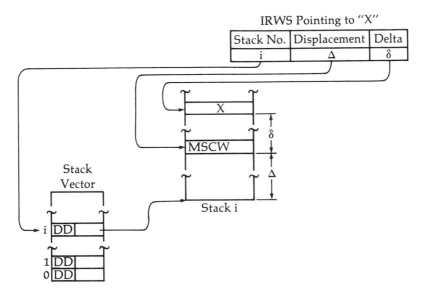

Figure 9.4 IRWS pointing to item "X."

start of the addressing space of a particular activation record within that stack, and (c) the displacement of the particular piece of information within that addressing space. Figure 9.4 illustrates this situation. Stuffed Indirect Reference Words may be used for addressing across stacks (i.e., between tasks) and for handling parameters, passed "by name" or "by reference," i.e., where the actual parameters are not necessarily within the addressing environment of the procedure to which they are passed and can therefore not be accessed via a (Display Register, Displacement) address couple.

9.4 STACK BUILD-UP AND PROCEDURE ENTRY

Consider the Algol program shown in Figure 9.5. Figure 9.6 shows the format of the job stack when line 3 of the program has been executed. Note the assignment of stack space for the real variables *R1* and *T1* (address couples 2, 2 and 2, 3) and for the Descriptor for array *A1* (address couple 2, 4). Note how the Descriptor for this two-dimensional array points to a space (outside the

Line
No.

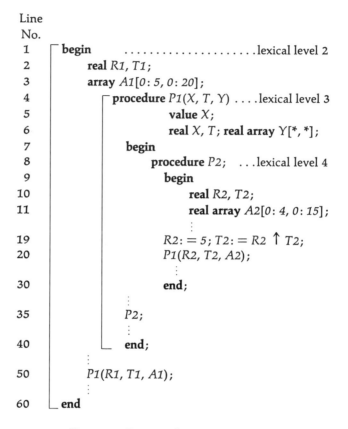

Figure 9.5 Program for Figures 9.6–9.11.

stack) containing one Descriptor for each row of the array. These latter Descriptors point to the actual space occupied by each row. (It should be remembered that this space can be in either primary or backup storage, i.e., in core or on the disk.)

Figure 9.6 demonstrates how information is entered into or extracted from the stacks. An Active Stack has the A, B, X, Y, and S registers and the stack limit (SL) and bottom of stack (BOS) registers of some processor associated with it. The X and Y registers may be regarded as double precision extensions of the A and B registers and will not be considered further. (See Table 9.1 for a

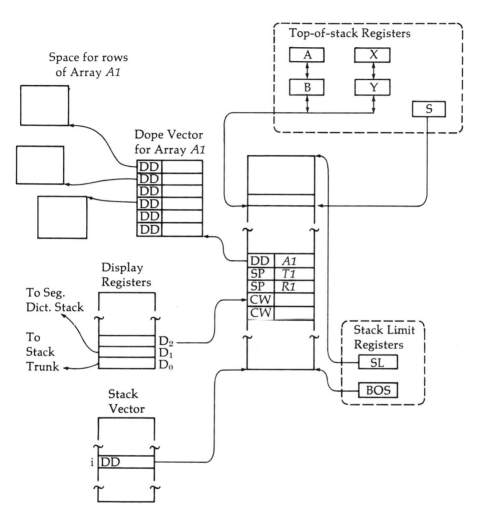

Figure 9.6 Stack i is the stack for the job associated with the program shown in Figure 9.5 (line 3). See Table 9.1 for an explanation of the tag notations used within words.

TABLE 9.1

EXPLANATION OF THE TAG NOTATIONS USED TO IDENTIFY
THE WORD TYPES IN FIGURES 9.6–9.15

Tag	Explanation
DD	Data descriptor
DDC	Copy descriptor
	(same as DD with copy bit *on*)
SP	Single precision
CW	Control word
IRW	Indirect reference word
IRWS	Stuffed indirect reference word
SD	Segment descriptor
PCW	Procedure control word
RCW	Return control word
MSCW	Mark stack control word
TOSCW	Top of stack control word

list of tag notations used to identify word types in Figures 9.6–
9.15.)

The stack operates as a last in, first out storage area. Thus an
operand is stored into register A with consequent push-downs into
register B and into the memory location pointed at by register S.
Similarly, extraction of data is from register A with consequent
pop-ups from B and the location referenced by S. The contents of
S are incremented by one on a push-down and decremented on a
pop-up. Should such an adjustment result in the S register's pointing at the bottom or top of stack (i.e., at the place pointed at by
either the BOS or SL register), an interrupt will occur and appropriate action will be taken.

Figure 9.7 illustrates the situation at line 19 in the program of
Figure 9.5. Procedures *P1* and *P2* have been entered, and procedure
P2 is now operating at level 4. The next line will call (recursively)
procedure *P1* whose declaration in the outer block is marked by a
Program Control Word (discussed below) accessed by the address
couple $(2, 5)$. Note how the three parameters for *P1* have been
passed, the value parameter (at 3, 2) directly, the real name parameter (at 3, 3) by means of an IRWS, and the array name parameter

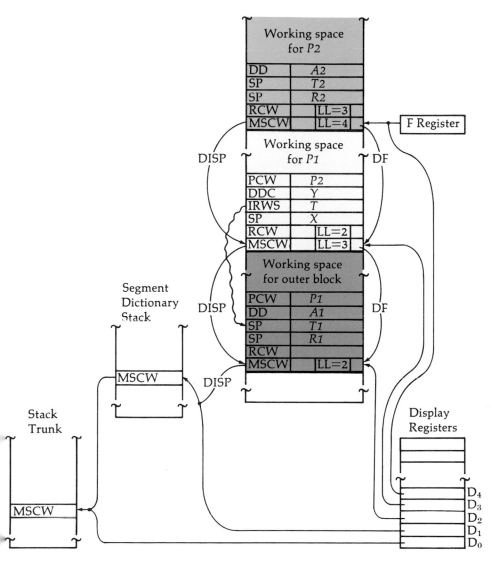

Figure 9.7 Showing the stack for the program of Figure 9.5 (line 19). The cell designated "Y" is a copy descriptor associated with the global array "A1."

by means of a descriptor that is a copy of the principal or "mom" descriptor found in the activation record of the outer block.

[Note the so-called "copy descriptor," whose mnemonic we have chosen as DDC, is distinguished by having its copy bit (field "C" in the descriptor format of Figure 9.2) *on*. In the B6700, copy descriptors point to their respective targets when the latter are in core, but point to their respective mom descriptors when the target is in auxiliary memory. Each time a target array is pushed out of core (or pulled into core) by the operating system, the affected copy descriptors, if any, as well as the mom descriptor are each properly altered to reflect the change in location of the target.

There has been some discussion among some of those familiar with B6700 architecture as to whether the copy descriptor should not *always*—i.e., irrespective of whether its target is in core or in auxiliary memory—point to its mom descriptor, and never directly to its target. The arguments on both sides should be apparent to the interested reader, and are in any case beyond the scope of this book. The copy descriptor is used extensively in circumstances other than those addressed in this section; the details, however, are unimportant to this discussion.]

A Mark Stack Control Word marks the start of the addressing space for each entered procedure. Each MSCW has a dynamic chain link (in its DF field) to the MSCW preceding it, and a static link (in its displacement field) to the MSCW that defines the immediately containing addressing environment. The DF chain of MSCW's thus forms the dynamic history of procedure entry. (It was referred to as the dc link in earlier chapters.) The LL field of the MSCW contains the lexical level of the procedure whose addressing space it marks. As each procedure is entered, appropriate Display Registers are set by the hardware. These Display Registers point at MSCW's and indicate the procedures (or blocks) whose addressing spaces are global to the procedure (or block) currently being entered. Similarly, on exit from a procedure, Display Registers may be reset to indicate a new addressing environment. The addressing space for the procedure whose code is currently being used by the process is pointed at both by a Display Register and by the F register (not shown previously).

Consider again Figure 9.7. Compilation of line 20 of the program

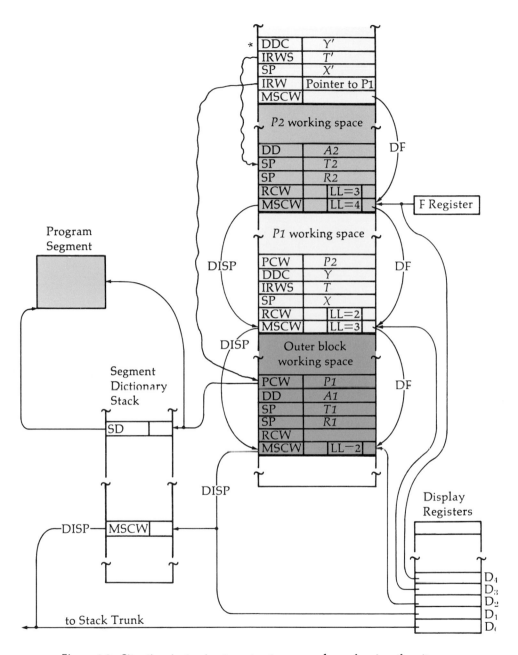

Figure 9.8 Situation just prior to entry to a procedure, showing the situation during execution of line 20 in the program of Figure 9.5. The cell designated "Y'" is a copy descriptor associated with the array *A2* declared locally in procedure *P2*.

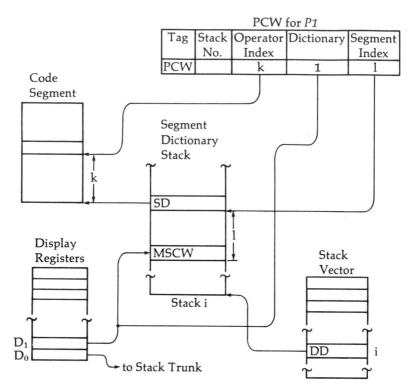

Figure 9.9 Showing how the Code Segment is accessed. The Stack Number field of the PCW is not shown.

of Figure 9.5 will generate the code necessary to call procedure *P1*. First of all, a skeleton MSCW is inserted in the stack. The skeleton MSCW (already) contains the DF field—namely, a copy of the content of the F register. Then a Normal or Stuffed IRW, pointing to the Procedure Control Word (PCW) for procedure *P1*, is constructed and pushed down onto the stack. Any actual parameters are pushed onto the stack. This situation is shown in Figure 9.8 where the relationship between IRW, PCW, Segment Descriptor and Code Segment (demonstrated in more detail in Figure 9.9) should be observed. Note particularly that the Segment Descriptor appears only once (there are never any copies) in the Segment Dictionary

Stack of the job. The term "Segment Dictionary Stack" should now be self-explanatory. Segment Descriptors can appear only at level 0 (in the Stack Trunk—i.e., for MCP procedures) or at level 1 (in the Segment Dictionary Stack). The stacks of two jobs that share a single Segment Dictionary will each contain a PCW for a particular procedure, but both PCW's will point to the same Segment Descriptor. If we add the condition that program code is "pure"—nonmodifiable—then the way in which re-entrancy is handled is clear [16].

At this point, the Enter operator will be encountered and the following (all achieved by Enter) will occur:

1. The F register will point at the newly inserted MSCW.

2. In order to create the addressing environment required by the procedure to be entered, i.e., in order to effect the correct "Display Update," it is necessary first to know the lexical level at which the procedure's PCW appears.

   (a) When the PCW is referenced by a Normal IRW, n is obtained directly from the address couple of that IRW. This is the case in the example where, since the IRW has the address couple $(2, 5)$, $n = 2$.

   (b) When the PCW is referenced by a Stuffed IRW, n is obtained from the LL field of the MSCW pointed at by the "$\triangle$" field of the IRWS (see Figure 9.4). Indeed, it is precisely with the objective of finding such an MSCW in mind that the IRWS structure is so contrived.

It should be noted that a procedure declared at level n must run at level $n + 1$; hence Display Register D_{n+1} is set to point at the newly inserted MSCW (i.e., Display Register D_{n+1} is set to the same value as the F register—see item 1 above). Also, the number $n + 1$ is inserted into the LL field of the MSCW. See Figure 9.10 which illustrates the case when $n = 2$.

When the PCW is referenced by an IRWS (note that this situation is not illustrated in the example), D_n is set to point at the MSCW from which n was determined. Such is not necessary when

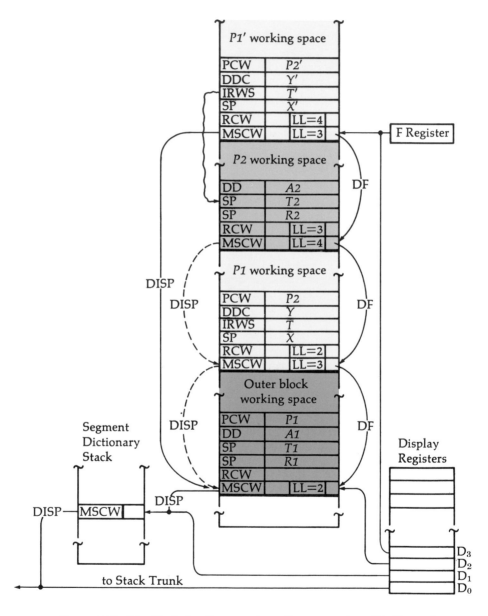

Figure 9.10 The Stack for the recursive call on procedure *P1*. Shows the situation just before start of execution of line 21 in the program of Figure 9.5.

the reference is via a normal IRW, since D_n is necessarily already set to the correct value for the new addressing environment.

3. The Stack Number and Displacement fields of the newly inserted MSCW are set to point to the MSCW pointed at by D_n (i.e., D_2 in the example).

We thus have a static link between MSCWs which expresses the lexical or contour structure of a program. In Burroughs literature this link is always referred to as the Displacement link. Static links may (as in Figure 9.8) parallel the dynamic links, but depart from the latter when recursive calls are encountered, or when disjoint procedures are called. See also Figure 3.5. The static link chains together a "nest" of procedures.

4. If necessary, the static or Displacement link in the MSCW pointed at by D_n (D_2 in the example) is examined and Display Register D_{n-1} is reset. The Displacement link is chased with consequent resetting of registers D_{n-2}, D_{n-3}, . . ., D_1 (D_0 is never reset) until all required registers have been reset. (Note: The Stack Number field in the Displacement link allows, if necessary, Display Registers to be reset across stacks—across families of tasks.) Such action is not required in the example since D_1 is already pointing at the correct MSCW and all lower Display Registers must consequently be set correctly for the procedure entry. Actually, the rule for termination of Display Update is a little more complicated than this, but the details are unimportant.

5. The newly inserted IRW or IRWS is changed to a "Return Control Word" (RCW). Note how the RCW (Figure 9.2) is very similar to the PCW and references the program code of the calling procedure, at one operator past the point of call, via a Segment Descriptor in much the same manner as illustrated in Figure 9.9. The LL field of the RCW contains the lexical level of the calling procedure.

The procedure has now been entered and is active. (The situation is shown in Figure 9.10 which is a display that is conceptually similar to Figure 3.2 but differs from it in degree of detail.) Its addressing environment is properly recorded, according to the rules of Algol, in the Display Registers. It has access to $T2$ and $A2$, which are outside its normal addressing environment, via the Stuffed Indirect Reference Word at $(3, 4)$ and via the copy descriptor which correspond to name parameters. Note that the new procedure has quite a different addressing environment from its caller and that Display Register 4, i.e., D_4, is no longer relevant. (The highest relevant Display Register for any processor is that which points to the same MSCW as the F register.) Figure 9.10 contains two sets of Displacement links—one active and associated with the called procedure and one passive and associated with the calling procedure. There may be many such sets within any stack.

On exit from a procedure, the DF link enables the MSCW associated with the calling procedure to be accessed. The LL field in the RCW (the Display level of the calling procedure) allows F and the topmost Display Register to be set. The Displacement linkages in the MSCW's, starting at that accessed by the new value of the F register, allow the Display Update to be effected. Finally, the code segment, and the next operator for the procedure exited to, are accessed via the RCW. Operation resumes at the point following the procedure call.

After such a procedure exit in the example, we are at line 21 in the program of Figure 9.5 and the situation is again very similar to that shown in Figure 9.7.

Figures 9.8–9.10 indicate how recursive calls on procedures are handled. In Figure 9.10 there are two activation records for procedure $P1$. The way in which Display Registers are manipulated at entry and exit ensures that the correct activation record—that associated with the most deeply nested call on the procedure—is always accessed for the addressing space of the procedure. For example, any reference to X, T, or Y in procedure $P1$ (in the example illustrated by Figure 9.10) will access X', T', or Y'. Note that the IRWS associated with T' accesses $T2$—i.e., accesses something outside the normal addressing environment of procedure $P1$. Likewise, the copy descriptor associated with Y' accesses the Dope Vector for $A2$, which is also outside the normal addressing environment of $P1$. This illustrates the usage of the IRWS and the copy descriptor in handling Algol "call-by-name" parameters.

9.5 HARDWARE INTERRUPTS

We have noted that interrupts are handled essentially as forced procedure calls. The interrupted processor adjusts the active stack with which it is associated. The effect is shown in Figure 9.11, which demonstrates an interrupt occurring immediately after the situation shown in Figure 9.10. The interrupted procedure appears to have called a system procedure, here called *int*, passing two parameters, *par1* and *par2*.

The interrupt procedure is written as part of the Operating System. Its PCW appears at a location (actually $D_0 + 3$) known to the hardware. Its function is to handle interrupts, whose natures are indicated by the parameters *par1* and *par2*, mostly by calling further system procedures which have been written to handle specific kinds of interrupts. On completion of interrupt handling, the Interrupt Procedure is exited like any other procedure: control thus returns to the point of interruption—the (theoretical) point of call.

9.6 MULTIPLE PROCESSORS

The B6700 may have more than one processor. Figure 9.12 demonstrates two jobs (A and B)—shown as reentrant for convenience —and running on two processors. It should be self explanatory.

9.7 JOB AND TASK INITIATION

To return to the earlier discussion of Figure 9.1. The ways in which jobs are "fired up" and the system switches a processor between jobs and/or tasks (between stacks [14]) have yet to be described. Henceforth we shall refer to different computations being made active or inactive as tasks, but since a task may be the main task of a job, we shall thereby incur no loss of generality.

Figure 9.13 shows the formats of an active and an inactive stack which represent, of course, an active and inactive task, respectively. It will be seen that the active stack is characterized by the presence of processor registers (Displays, F, SL, S and BOS) which point into it and by the fact that the lowest word in the stack is a single pre-

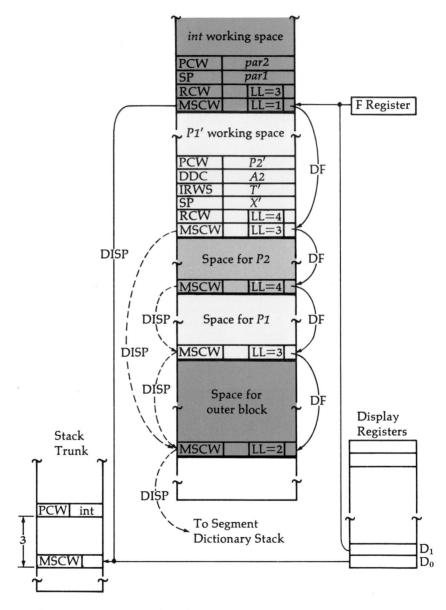

Figure 9.11   Interrupted stack format. An interrupt has occurred immediately following the situation shown in Figure 9.10, i.e., just before the start of execution of line 21 in the program of Figure 9.5.

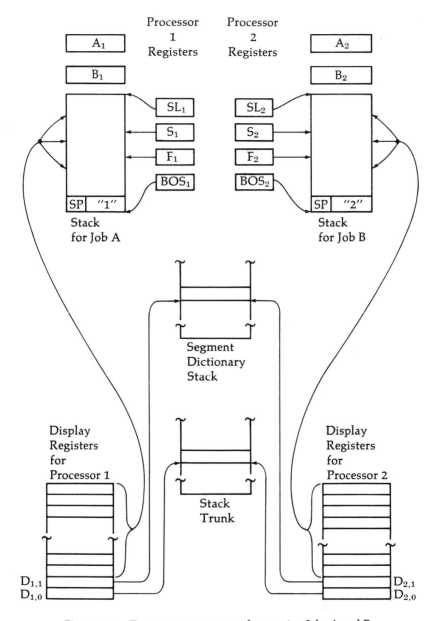

Figure 9.12 Two-processor system for running Jobs A and B.

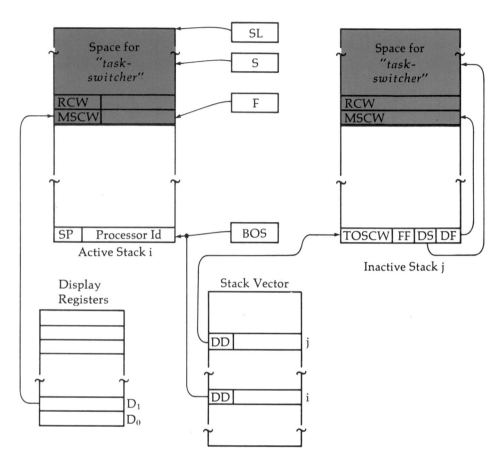

Figure 9.13 Active and inactive stacks.

cision operand (i.e., with a tag of 0) containing a number which uniquely identifies the processor. There are no processor registers pointing into the inactive stack, and its first word is a so-called Top-of-Stack Control Word (TOSCW).

It will be recalled that all stacks are linked into the Stack Vector and that each stack is uniquely identified by its Stack Number. To switch a processor between tasks, the active task has merely to issue (in a higher level language) such statements as Continue(New-

Task). New-Task is a task identifier which translates ultimately to a Stack Number. The compilation of such a Continue statement produces machine code of the form Mvst(nt), where Mvst represents the Move Stack machine operator and nt is the Stack Number corresponding to the task identified by New-Task.

[Note: The switching between jobs and MCP tasks (as distinct from the switching between user tasks) is a little different from that implied by such as Continue statements. However, the differences are not important.]

The TOSCW contains—as will be seen in Figure 9.13—pointers to the settings of the S and F registers (actually these pointers [DS and DF] are in the form of offsets to allow for relocatability of stacks), at the time the task last went inactive, together with the settings of various flip-flops (FF) at that time.

The switching of control between tasks is accomplished by a system procedure—called *"task-switcher"* in the diagram. The call on the procedure is generated when a compiler sees a statement such as the Continue statement. The last two operators in the code stream for task switches are Mvst and Exit. Exit is the operator generated by the terminating "End" of the procedure. The Mvst operator does the following: (1) stores pointers to the S and F register settings and various flip-flop settings in the first word of the active stack (shown as stack i in Figure 9.13); (2) changes the tag of the first word—it is no longer a single-precision operand but is now a TOSCW; (3) sets the S and F registers and various flip-flops from the fields in the TOSCW of the inactive stack (shown as stack j in Figure 9.13); (4) sets the first word in this stack to a Single Precision Operand containing the value of the processor ID; and (5) sets the BOS and SL registers from element j of the Stack Vector.

At this point, the previously active stack is now inactive and the previously inactive stack is active. It is important to understand that the newly active stack was previously rendered inactive by an exactly equivalent swapping. Hence, the Exit operator next encountered will cause an exit from *task-switcher* into the procedure of the newly active task that contained the Continue statement responsible for its deactivation. It should be appreciated that all the mechanisms of procedure exit—Display Update and correct code access—as described earlier are set in motion and that therefore the newly active task will proceed to operate at the point of its previous deactivation.

It should be further appreciated that the newly inactive task is now a candidate for reactivation via a (Mvst, Exit) operator pair issued by some other task. The mechanism is perfectly symmetrical.

There still remains the question of how jobs and tasks are first presented to the system. Figure 9.14 demonstrates this situation for a Job. The system builds a Segment Dictionary and a Job Stack and links the Job Stack into the queue of tasks ready to run. There are two activation records in the Job Stack. The lowest one is for a system procedure called *run*. The stack is made to look as if a named parameter, referring to the PCW for the outer block of the task to be initiated has been passed to *run*.

When the task is chosen from the queue of tasks ready to run, some other task issues a [Mvst(nt), Exit] pair, as described above, where nt is the Stack Number of the new stack. The effect is to cause the system procedure *run* to be entered (actually to be exited to; the topmost activation record in the job stack is a dummy record). *Run* is coded to call the outer block of the new task. Hence, the final effect is as shown in Figure 9.15.

When the task eventually terminates, an exit takes place, in the normal manner, to the procedure *run*. *Run* is therefore the primary system procedure for initiation and termination of tasks. It can take care of all the accounting and housekeeping functions. Like all other procedures, *run* is re-entrant and therefore has only one code segment even though all tasks have their lowest activation record associated with *run*.

If a task terminates abnormally, then the expected exit from its outermost block into procedure *run* will not occur. In this case, the system generates a "Go-To," from the procedure where the abnormality is detected, into *run*. Such a Go-To, sometimes called a Bad-Go-To, is implemented in a manner which will not be described, such that all activation records above that for *run* appear to have been exited in the normal manner. [Note: Bad-Go-To's to procedures other than *run*, i.e., those not associated with abnormalities, are also handled in this manner.] Hence, the final effect is as if the outer block had been exited in the normal manner. *Run*, how-

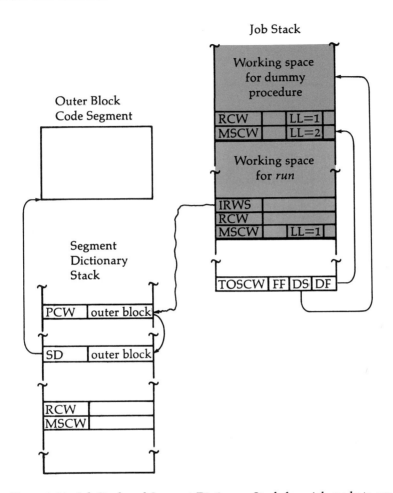

Figure 9.14 Job Stack and Segment Dictionary Stack for a job ready to run. Note that Job Stack is linked into a queue of tasks that are ready to run. Queue linkages are not shown.

ever, which is aware of the abnormal condition, can take action appropriate to the particular abnormality.

The above is primarily concerned with the activation of, and switching between, MCP tasks and the initial tasks of jobs. Only scant mention has been made of tasks—such as coroutines—which

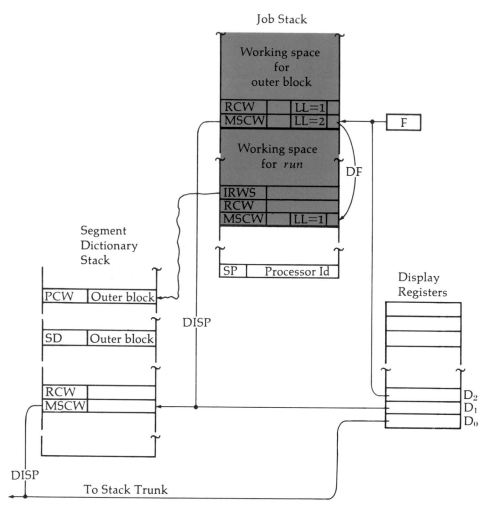

Figure 9.15 Job Stack and Segment Dictionary Stack for a job which has just started running. Only active displacement links are shown.

have been created by other tasks via syntactical structures in higher level applications languages (e.g., B6700 Algol [12]). It turns out that all tasks, whether they be "primary" or offspring, are initiated and terminated utilizing the procedure *run* as described in this section. All tasks are deactivated and reactivated using the system procedure *task-switcher* again as described in this section. The ways in which an offspring task may access variables in its ancestors—via Display Registers is described primarily in Chapter 4. At various points in the text it was pointed out how the mechanism of Display Update, as described in Section 9.4 is involved in switching between tasks and how this mechanism effects the change of addressing environment necessitated by such a switch. Such remarks are again applicable to all tasks no matter what their origin. Section 9.3 describes the use of the Stuffed Indirect Reference Word in addressing across stacks—across tasks—and again it will be seen how the nature of such tasks is unimportant to the discussion.

In short, tasks are handled in a perfectly uniform and general manner. When this is realized, the ways in which the mechanisms described in this chapter (and discussed in connection with a fairly trivial task family) are appropriate to the handling of complex situations should be readily understood.

Bibliography

1. Abrams, P. S., "An APL Machine," Stanford Electronics Labs., Tech. Rept. No. 3, February 1970.
2. Barton, R. S., "A New Approach to the Functional Design of a Digital Computer," *Proc. West. Joint Computer Conf., 1961*, May 9–11, pp. 393–396, Western Joint Computer Conference, Los Angeles, California.
3. Barton, R. S., "Ideas for Computer Systems Organization: A Personal Survey," in "Software Engineering" (COINS III) (J. T. Tou, ed.), Vol. 1, pp. 7–16, Academic Press, New York, 1970.
4. Bernstein, A. J., Detlefsen, G. D., and Kerr, R. H., "Process Control and Communication," *Proc. ACM Symp. Operating Systems Principles, 2nd, Princeton Univ., October 1969*, pp. 83–91, Association for Computing Machinery, New York.
5. Berry, D. M., "Block Structure: Retention or Deletion?" Center for Computer and Information Science, Brown Univ., Tech. Rept., 70–29, December 1970.
6. Berry, D. M., "Introduction to Oregano" (*ACM SIGPLAN Symp. on Data Structures in Programming Languages, Univ. of Florida, Gainesville, February 1971*), *SIGPLAN Notices* 6 (2), 171–190.
7. Brown, J. S., "A Generalization of APL," Ph.D. Dissertation, Dept. Systems and Information Science, Syracuse Univ., New York, 1971.
8. The Burroughs Corp., "B6500 System Reference Manual (001)," The Burroughs Corp., Detroit, Michigan, Form No. 1043676, September 1969.
9. The Burroughs Corp., "B6700 Data Communications Extended Algol Information Manual," The Burroughs Corp., Detroit, Michigan, Form No. 5000052, August 1971.
10. The Burroughs Corp., "The Descriptor—a definition of the B5000 Information Processing System," The Burroughs Corp., Detroit, Michigan, Bull. No. 5000-20002-P, February 1961.

11. The Burroughs Corp., "B6700 Espol Reference Manual," The Burroughs Corp., Detroit, Michigan, Form No. 5000094, November 1970.

12. The Burroughs Corp., "Extended Algol Reference Manual," The Burroughs Corp., Detroit Michigan, Form No. 5000128, July 1971.

13. The Burroughs Corp., "Master Control Program Reference Manual," The Burroughs Corp., Detroit, Michigan, Form No. 1042447, February 1970.

14. The Burroughs Corp., "A Narrative Description of the B5500 Disk File Control Program," The Burroughs Corp., Detroit, Michigan, Form No. 1023579, October 1969.

15. Chesley, G. D., and Smith, W. R., "The Hardware-Implemented High-Level Machine Language for SYMBOL," *AFIPS Conf. Proc.* **38**, 563–573 (1971). AFIPS Press, Montvale, New Jersey.

16. Cleary, J. G., "Process Handling on Burroughs B6500," *Proc. Australian Computer Conf., 4th, Adelaide, S. Australia, August 1969*, pp. 231–239.

17. "The Generation Gap," Part 1, *Computer World*, p. 9, April 25 (1969); part 2. *ibid.*, p. 9, April 30 (1969) Part 3. *ibid.*, May 7 (1969).

18. Corbató, F. J., and Vyssotsky, V. A., "Introduction and Overview of the Multics System, *Proc. AFIPS 1965 Fall Joint Computer Conf.* **27**, Part 1, 185–196 (1965). Spartan Books, New York.

19. Cosine Committee, Commission on Education, "An Undergraduate Course on Operating System Principles," Rept. of Task Force VIII, pp. 24–28, Washington, D.C., June 1971.

20. Cowart, B. E., Rice, R., and Lundstrom, S. F., "The Physical Attributes and Testing Aspects of the SYMBOL System," *AFIPS Conf. Proc.* **38**, 589–600, (1971). AFIPS Press, Montvale, New Jersey.

21. Creech, B. A., "Architecture of the B6500," in "Software Engineering" (COINS III) (J. T. Tou, ed.), Vol. 1, pp. 29–43. Academic Press, New York, 1970.

22. Davis, G. M. "The English Electric KDF9 Computer System," *Comp. Bull.* **4** (3), 119–120 (1960).

23. Denning, P. J., "Virtual Memory," *ACM Comput. Surveys* **2** (3), 153–189 (1970).

24. Dennis, J. B., and Van Horn, E. C., "Programming Semantics for Multiprogrammed Computations" (*ACM Programming Languages and Pragmatics Conf., San Dimas, California, August 1965*), *Comm. ACM* **9** (3), 143–155 (1966).

25. Dijkstra, E. W., "An ALGOL 60 Translator for the X1 Computer," Algol Bull. Suppl. No. 10 (1960) [Transl. from the German in *MTW* **2**, 54–56 (1961); *MTW* **3**, 115–119 (1961).

26. Dijkstra, E. W., "Cooperating Sequential Processes," Chapter 2 in "Programming Languages" (F. Genuys, Ed.), Academic Press, New York and London, 1968.

27. Dijkstra, E. W., "The Structure of 'THE' Multiprogramming System," *Comm. ACM* **11** (5), 341–346, (1968).

28. Graham, R. M., "Protection in an Information Processing Utility," *Comm. ACM* **11** (5), 365–369 (1968).

29. Hansen, P. B., "A Comparison of Two Synchronizing Concepts," *Acta Informatica* **1**, 190–199 (1972).

30. Hansen, P. B., "The Nucleus of a Multiprogramming System," *Comm. ACM*, **13** (4), 238–241; 250 (1970).

31. Hassitt, A., Lageschulte, J. W., and Lyon, L. E., "Implementation of a High-Level Language Machine," IBM Scientific Center, 4th Annual Workshop on Microprogramming, Univ. of California, Santa Cruz, September 1971.

32. Hauck, E. A., and Dent, B. A., "Burroughs' B6500/7500 Stack Mechanism," *Proc. AFIPS 1968 Spring Joint Computer Conf.* **32**, 245–251 (1968). Thompson, Washington. D.C.

33. Hoare, C. A. R., "Towards a Theory of Parallel Programming," *Internat. Symp. Operating System Techniques, Belfast, N. Ireland, August–September 1971.*

34. IBM Systems Reference Library, "PL/1 Language Specification," revised ed. IBM Systems Reference Library, Form No. C28-6571, 1966.

35. Iliffe, J. K., "Basic Machine Principles," Macdonald, London and Amer. Elsevier, New York, 1968.

36. Iverson, K. E., "A Programming Language," Wiley, New York, 1962.

37. Johnston, J. B., "The Contour Model of Block Structured Processes" (*ACM SIGPLAN Symp. on Data Structures in Programming Languages, Univ. of Florida, Gainesville, February 1971*), *SIGPLAN Notices* **6** (2), 55–82, February 1971).

38. Johnston, J. B., "Structure of Multiple Activity Algorithms," *Proc. Ann. Princeton Conf. on Inform. Sci. and Systems, 3rd, Princeton, March 1969*, pp. 38–43.

39. Lampson, B. W., "A Scheduling Philosophy for Multiprocessing Systems," (*ACM Symp. on Operating System Principles, 1st, Gatlinburg, Tenn., October 1967*). *Comm. ACM* **11** (5), 347–360 (1968).

40. Lampson, B. W., "Dynamic Protection Structures." *AFIPS Conf. Proc.* **35**, 27–38 (1969), AFIPS Press, Montvale, New Jersey.

41. Don M. Lyle, "A Hierarchy of High Order Languages for Systems Programming," (*Proc. SIGPLAN Symp. on Languages for Systems Implementation, Purdue University, October 1971*), *SIGPLAN Notices* **6** (9), 73–78 (1971).

42. Mealy, G. H., Witt, B. I., and Clark, W. A., "The Functional Structure of OS/360," *IBM Systems J.* **5** (1), 1–51 (1966).

43. Morris, D., and Detlefsen, G. D., "A Virtual Processor for Real Time Operations," in "Software Engineering" (COINS III) (J. T. Tou, Ed.), Vol. 1, pp. 17–28, Academic Press, New York, 1970.

44. Nauer, P. *et al.*, "Revised Report on the Algorithmic Language ALGOL 60," *Comm. ACM* **6** (1), 1–17 (1963).

45. Newman, W. M., Gouraud, H., and Oestreicher, D. R., "A Programmer's

Guide to PDP-10 Euler," Div. of Computer Science, Univ. of Utah, Salt Lake City, Tech. rept. UTEC-CSc-70-105, June 1970.

46. Organick, E. I., "The Multics System: An Examination of its Structure," MIT Press, Cambridge, Masaschusetts, 1972.

47. Organick, E. I., and Cleary, J. G., "A Data Structure Model of the B6700 Computer System," (*ACM SIGPLAN Symp. on Data Structures in Programming Languages, Univ. of Florida, Gainesville, February 1971*), *SIGPLAN Notices* **6** (2), 83–145 (1971).

48. Patel, R. M., "Basic I/O Handling on Burroughs B6500." *Proc. ACM Symp. on Operating System Principles, 2nd., Princeton Univ., October 1969*, pp. 120–129.

49. Randell, B., and Kuehner, C. J., "Dynamic Storage Allocation Systems," *Comm. ACM* **11** (5), 297–306 (1968).

50. Randell, B., and Russell, L. J., "ALGOL 60 Implementation," Academic Press, New York, 1964.

51. Reynolds, J. C., "GEDANKEN, A Simple Typeless Language Based on the Principle of Completeness and the Reference Concept," *Comm. ACM* **13** (5), 308–319 (1970).

52. Rice University Research Staff, "Rice Computer-2 General Specifications," Dept. Electrical Engineering, Rice Univ., Houston, Texas, September 1970. Also Feustal, E. A., "The Rice Research Computer," *AFIPS Conf. Proc.* **40**, 369–377 (1972), AFIPS, Montvale, New Jersey.

53. Rice, R., and Smith, W. R., "SYMBOL—A Major Departure from Classic Software Dominated von Neumann Computing Systems," *AFIPS Conf. Proc.* **38**, 575–581 (1971). AFIPS, Montvale, New Jersey.

54. Saltzer, J. H., "Traffic Control in a Multiplexed Computer System," Sc. D. Thesis, Dept. Electrical Engineering, MIT, Cambridge, Massachusetts, May 1966: Also Project MAC Tech. Rept. TR-30, July 1966, 79 pp.

55. Smith, W. R., *et al.*, "SYMBOL—A Large Experimental System Exploring Major Hardware Replacement of Software," *AFIPS Conf. Proc.* **38**, 601–616, (1971), AFIPS, Montvale, New Jersey.

56. Spier, M. J., and Organick, E. I., "The Multics Interprocess Communication Facility," *Proc. ACM Symp. on Operating Systems Principles, 2nd, Princeton Univ., October 1969*, pp. 83–91.

57. Thurber, K. J., and Myrna, J. W., "System Design of a Cellular APL Computer," *IEEE Trans. Electronic Computers* **EC-19** (4), 291–303 (1970).

58. Wegner, P., "Data Structure Models for Programming Languages" (*ACM SIGPLAN Symp. on Data Structures in Programming Languages, Univ. of Florida, Gainesville, February 1971*), *SIGPLAN Notices* **6** (2), 1–54 (1971).

59. Weizer, N., and Oppenheimer, G., "Virtual Memory Management in a Paging Environment," *Proc. AFIPS 1969 Spring Joint Computer Conf.* **34**, 249–256 (1969), AFIPS, Montvale, New Jersey.

60. Van Wijngaarden, A. (Ed.), Maillou, B. J., Peck, J. E. L., and Koster, C. H. A., "Report on the Algorithmic Language ALGOL 68," Math. Center,

Amsterdam Rept. MR101, Amsterdam, October 1969. Also ACM, New York.

61. Wirth, N. and Weber, H., "EULER: A Generalization of ALGOL and its Formal Definition," *Comm. ACM* **9** (1), 13–23 (1966); *ibid.* **9** (2), 89–99 (1966).

62. Wozencraft, J. M., and Evans, A., "Notes on Programming Linguistics," Dept. Electrical Engineering, MIT, Cambridge, Massachusetts, July 1969.

Index